Good Content

A Genuine Content Strategy for the
Reluctant Marketer

Stanley Idesis

Good Content

A Genuine Content Strategy for the Reluctant Marketer

Stanley Idesis

ISBN 978-1-7324057-2-1

Leanpub

This is a Leanpub book. Leanpub empowers authors and publishers with the Lean Publishing process. Lean Publishing is the act of publishing an in-progress ebook using lightweight tools and many iterations to get reader feedback, pivot until you have the right book and build traction once you do.

A huge, Venti-sized thank you to everyone who made this possible: Forsyth, Erin, Fred, David, Stoyan, Misha, dad, and Beau-Beau for putting up with my incessant typing.

And a heart-felt thank you to Simona; she transformed a 'some day' promise into a 'today' reality. That is one of the (many) reasons I love you.

Contents

Why Content Marketing

"Content marketing is the only marketing left."

– Seth Godin, Author, Entrepreneur, and TED Speaker

As a former code school educator, I created Android and iOS courses, built mobile applications, mentored students, and got along happily unaware of content marketing. On an odd day in 2015, courses were done, apps written, and students mentored; my teammates and I had a large pile of nothing on our plates. Our leaders aimed our idle hands at growth: *have them answer questions on Quora*, they strongly suggested.

Quora was and is a social media platform that surfaces the best answers to any question one so bravely poses of its users. Chance brought thousands of code school prospects to this platform in search of reviews, opinions, and dirty gossip behind popular code school options. Our higher-ups tasked us to seek out relevant questions and provide thoughtful answers (alongside links to our marketing materials, of course).

As I drafted answers to questions about Java, Android, iOS, and learning, I compared my works-in-progress to responses submitted by our competitors: I spotted a sour trend in their writing. Our competitors used these questions as opportunities to boast and advocate exclusively their services; the stink of self-promotion wafted like noxious gas. Instead of answering the questions to the best of their knowledge, they offered their products as solutions to the questions—they advertised.

As I read these attempts to pass advertising off as content, I became spiritually in-tune with my personal aversion to bull... ahem, *shenanigans*. False answers inspired my distrust and tarnished the reputation of both the brand that produced them and its online representative. If these answers inspired those feelings within me, so would they in Quora's readers. To prevent our brand from suffering the same fate, I vowed to write earnestly and with minimal self-promotion. That vow changed my career.

My answers shot above the egotism and chest-beating with honesty, vulnerability, and an equal assessment of options. I treated our competitors with respect and showed our potential students alternatives that could save them money. I advised students to consider our competitors or worse, teach themselves. Doing so enabled students to skip the code school process entirely; a choice that inevitably led to lost sales.

You may be wondering, *what kind of backwards marketing team would green-light this content?* Not ours. As part of curriculum development, I had full creative control over my writing, and my creativity called for candor. I was certain my brazen honesty would win the company a total of zero prospects, but I was proud to satisfy the marketing team's requests while maintaining integrity as a writer. To the surprise of my team, my manager, and especially myself, Operation Earnest paid off. Big time.

At our team's peak, 1 of every 10 new students found us through Quora. *What?* But the growing number of prospects was only one side-effect of our approach. The conquering of Quora convinced the marketing team that curriculum authors should write blog posts as well; these posts would speak to similar concerns voiced by Quora users. One blog in particular compared four code schools in Los Angeles, my then-current residence. I was a perfect match for the post and we published my piece unceremoniously.

One month later, a startling email arrived in my company inbox: a praise-filled letter from the competition. The email's author had just enrolled a student at his Los Angeles code school. This student discovered the author's school after reading a blog post, my blog post. The author expressed his gratitude for my even-handed comparison and before signing off, he invited me to a coding meet-up hosted by his company.

Dozens of prospective students attended his meet-up each week and he wanted me to join and promote my organization. He planned not to mock me, humiliate me, or pummel me with tomatoes vaudeville-style. Instead, he wanted to publicize my company (his direct competitor) to the prospective leads he worked tirelessly to attract. That exchange taught me the power of honest, helpful, and respectful content. Good content.

Good content inspires trust in your organization and the consideration of your services by people who respect you before they meet you. And respect is a difficult thing to earn in an online world teeming with false news sources and advertising that poses as truth. And you can learn to create exceptional content that preserves your integrity, generates revenue, and delights your target audience by reading this book.

Do better books on content marketing exist? Yes. Have authors with more clout covered these topics? Of course. But will any be as honest, open, and direct with you as this one? **Hell, no.** Let's cut the *shenanigans* and get to marketing.[1]

---

[1]And if you think most content marketing *is* shenanigans, I want to show you a better way.

Use This Book

Before we get started with the material, I want to help you make full use of this book. The book has three exercises within: skip them. You can do the exercises as they appear of course, but I recommend you complete the book before you attempt them. After reading the material, you will have a better understanding of how the exercises work together to help you achieve your business goals.

I've placed the exercises where they make pedagogical sense (they follow the section that introduces them). But you will gain the most from these drills by performing them one after another in sequence. However, you're an adult and my advice, like all advice, is merely that. Feel free to enjoy the book as you see fit, just as long as you enjoy it.

Definitions

When you come across a footnote like this one, $42^?$, the ? symbol indicates a definition found in the glossary. I suggest you jump to the glossary to quickly skim the definition before you continue reading.

Conquer Prerequisites

I love it when 10-pages in, a book directs me to other books; but I know some don't share that unique passion of mine. Thankfully, we can learn a lot from this text without familiarizing ourselves with the recommendations below. However, implementing this book's strategy to its fullest requires each skill (or employing someone who possesses it).

Some believe that the cornerstone of a great content strategy is writing, and to a large degree they are correct. Writing forms the backbone of all content, but without the proper tools to analyze and track the content's performance, this strategy is half-baked. That is why writing finds its place at the top of this list, but equally important skills are hot on its heels.

1. Writing

How often do we consider our own writing? Is it fast and loose? Error-free? Littered with grammatical mischief? Regardless of our writing's condition, it can improve. I was an amateur writer myself until my previous role forced me to focus on pencraft. From sentence structure to word choice, how we write impacts the quality and staying-power of our content. Remember this famous quote?

> *"Like, don't ask your country what it can do for you, man. But think real hard about what you might be able to do for it, you know...?"*
>
> *"...Thanks."*
>
> – John F. Kennedy

I don't remember that either because the 35th president of the United States never uttered that drivel. If JFK eked out that clunky mess of a sentence instead of his eloquent phrasing, history would have crumpled that speech up and tossed it into the cultural scrap heap. Luckily for us, Kennedy had top speech writers.

Suggested Tools
Grammarly[2]

Hemingway Editor[3]

Suggested Reading
On Writing Well: An Informal Guide to Writing Non-fiction[4] by William Zinsser

---

[2]https://www.grammarly.com/
[3]http://www.hemingwayapp.com/
[4]https://amzn.to/2pVFAw3

The Elements of Style[5] by William Strunk Jr. and E. B. White

Bare Minimum

To develop their style and enhance their vocabulary, great writers read the works of great authors. At the least, content marketers should read one piece of classic literature per year.

---

[5]https://amzn.to/2H11oO1

2. Spreadsheets

The invention of the spreadsheet revolutionized the finance industry and according to Steve Jobs, spreadsheets, "[were] what propelled the Apple II to the success it achieved." Spreadsheets gave people a reason to buy the world's first computers. 40 years later the spreadsheet remains a central piece in the relationship between man and machine. What I'm trying to say is, if we plan to utilize computers (and this strategy) to its fullest, we must understand spreadsheets.

This strategy uses spreadsheets to track planned content, individual content pieces, their performance, and more. While this information is often stored within the tools we use to gather it (SEMRush, AdWords Keyword Planner, Search Console, others), spreadsheets provide an easy-to-share, no-cost method to access important data without leaving it trapped in a 3rd party database.

Suggested Tools
> Google Sheets[6]
>
> Microsoft Excel[7]
>
> OpenOffice Calc[8]

Suggested Free Resources
> Sheets — Google Learning Center[9]
>
> Excel Help Center[10]

---

[6] https://www.google.com/sheets/about/

[7] https://products.office.com/en-us/excel

[8] https://www.openoffice.org/product/calc.html

[9] https://gsuite.google.com/learning-center/products/sheets/#!/

[10] https://support.office.com/en-us/excel

Suggested Coursework

Master Google Sheets[11]

Excel Quick Start Tutorial: 36 Minutes to Learn the Basics[12]

Bare Minimum

Learn how a spreadsheet tracks data by row and column. Generally, each row acts as an 'entry' and each column a data point found on that entry. If one can recreate a shopping list in a spreadsheet, they can take full advantage of this text.

As a bonus, one should learn to import a Comma-Separated Values (CSV)? file into a spreadsheet.

---

[11] https://www.udemy.com/google-spreadsheet-tutorial/
[12] https://www.udemy.com/excel_quickstart/

3. Web Analytics

At the heart of a successful online business beats the drum of analytics. Analytics helps site owners track usage behavior, sales funnels, conversion rates, and more. For content strategies, analytics calculates the success of a strategy or piece of content and whether it contributes to the bottom line. Without an underlying analytics platform, publishing a piece of content is shooting in the dark.

Suggested Tool
  Google Analytics[13]

Suggested Free Resource
  Analytics Academy[14]

Suggested Reading
  Learning Google AdWords and Google Analytics[15] by Benjamin Mangold

  Google Analytics Breakthrough: From Zero to Business Impact[16] by Feras Alhlou

Suggested Coursework
  Google Analytics Training Course for Beginners[17]

Bare Minimum
  One should learn to create a Google Analytics web property, connect it to their website (possible HTML editing required), create Goals?, and navigate predefined Reports?.

---

[13]http://analytics.google.com
[14]https://analytics.google.com/analytics/academy/
[15]https://amzn.to/2q6Wt76
[16]https://amzn.to/2Jsbusa
[17]https://www.udemy.com/google-analytics-insights/

4. Webmaster Tools

The world's major search engines, Google and Bing, provide site owners with critical traffic information. Using these tools, we can learn how people find our site, how often they click, where we rank among key search terms, and more. Without this data we struggle to bolster our strengths and minimize our weaknesses. Thankfully, these tools are relatively easy to incorporate and learn.

Required Tools
Google Search Console[18]
Bing Webmaster Tools[19]

Suggested Free Resources
How to use Google and Bing webmaster tools for beginners[20]

Getting Started Checklist - Bing Webmaster Tools[21]

Search Engine Optimization (SEO) Starter Guide[22]

Suggested Coursework
Onsite SEO Using Google Search Console-Webmaster Tools[23]

Bare Minimum
Readers should claim their website on both tools

---

[18]https://www.google.com/webmasters/tools/home?hl=en

[19]https://www.bing.com/toolbox/webmaster

[20]https://www.reliablesoft.net/how-to-use-google-and-bing-webmaster-tools-for-beginners/

[21]https://www.bing.com/webmaster/help/getting-started-checklist-66a806de

[22]https://support.google.com/webmasters/answer/7451184

[23]https://www.udemy.com/onsite-seo-using-google-search-console-webmaster-tools/

(DNS editing required) and understand how to gather
Page Rank data—discussed later.

5. Working With Websites

We needn't understand how to setup servers, manage a shopping cart, design a beautiful layout, and code every page by hand—even I wouldn't do all that. But I recommend that we understand how to modify the internal workings of our website. The skills required to do so depend on how our site is built, assuming we already have one.

If we don't have a site, free and affordable Content Management Systems (CMS)? like Squarespace and Word-Press are great places to start.

Suggested Tools

 HTML5?

 JavaScript?

 Squarespace[24]

 WordPress[25]

Suggested Free Resources

 W3 Schools[26]

 Getting Started with Squarespace[27]

 Tutorials and Courses for Beginners – Learn Word-Press[28]

Suggested Reading

 HTML and CSS: Design and Build Websites[29] by Jon Duckett

---

[24] https://www.squarespace.com/

[25] https://wordpress.org/

[26] https://www.w3schools.com/

[27] https://support.squarespace.com/hc/en-us/articles/205809798-Video-Series-Getting-Started-with-Squarespace

[28] https://learn.wordpress.com/

[29] https://amzn.to/2uD89CX

Suggested Coursework

Codecademy[30]

Complete WordPress Training For Beginners[31]

Bare Minimum

Content marketers must have access to edit the navigational elements (top-level) pages of their website both on mobile and desktop. They must also be capable of editing the URLs, titles, descriptions, and contents of all pages. More on those later.

---

[30]https://www.codecademy.com/catalog/language/html-css
[31]https://www.udemy.com/complete-wordpress-course-for-beginners/

6. Search Engine Optimization

Search Engine Optimization (SEO) is a broad topic that incorporates all three subjects that precede it, so we've placed it last. In this book we cover fundamental SEO topics such as keywords, ranking factors, and meta data— the remainder is an overwhelming swamp obsessed with minutiae. SEO professionals see themselves as Gods among men capable of reversing the course of doomed ventures with link building and Black Hat[?] tactics; as reputable business people, we ignore their duplicitous promises.

Take note, *no single person at Google understands how their search engine works*, so how can anyone else expect to? Understanding a bit past the basics will get us 80% of the way there, and that's more than enough.

Suggested Tools
SEMRush[32]

SEOMoz[33]

Suggested Free Resource
SEO Training Course by Moz[34]

Suggested Reading
SEO 2018: Learn search engine optimization with smart internet marketing strategies[35] by Adam Clarke

SEO Fitness Workbook: 2018 Edition: The Seven Steps to Search Engine Optimization Success on Google[36] by Jason McDonald

---

[32]https://www.semrush.com/
[33]https://moz.com/
[34]https://www.udemy.com/whiteboard-seo/
[35]https://amzn.to/2GqyrOz
[36]https://amzn.to/2pS2W5K

Bare Minimum

As this book will detail, the content of each web page signals its purpose to search engines. Content marketers must understand that a page's ranking among those with similar purpose is strongly based on the quality of that content, the level to which it satisfies the visitor, the number of trustworthy websites pointing to that page, and the internal structure of the page (often managed by our CMS).

Recap

This book introduces and defines concepts found among these subject matters, but assumes readers can go beyond to learn the skills and apply them in practice.

Without a bare minimum competency in these abilities (or lack thereof among staff), implementing this book's strategy to its utmost is unfortunately impossible.

Define 'Good'

More than any piece of advice found in this book, the suggestion to write *good content* is the toughest to absorb. In the previous sections we encountered a brief introduction to what I perceive as good content, now let me elaborate. I believe that a piece of content falls on a spectrum that begins at *good* and ends at *guile*.

Guile

The skillful use of dishonest means to trick people or make them do what you want.

– Macmillan Dictionary

At the far end we have click-bait headlines and derivative material, plagiarized from a dozen credible sources, so thinly diluted that it borders on meaninglessness. Guile lacks novel ideas, thoughts, and serves the purpose of one: the publisher. Guile is easy to forget, but if retained, leaves a bad impression on the reader. Good content does the opposite.

Good content provides value, delivers on the promise of its headline, and does so by placing the focus on the reader. Whereas guile serves our needs, good content serves the reader's needs, the customer's needs. The majority of content produced by respectable brands falls somewhere in the middle; this happens for two reasons.

First, readers have grown accustomed to click-bait and to see it for what it truly is: valueless drivel. Quality

brands are smart to avoid publishing click-bait garbage—
but do they produce *good content?* Brands lean to content that delivers information in a way that reinforces
their value proposition but diminishes criticism. This
middle-spectrum is what we'll call *safe content.*

Fear motivates brands to write safe content. Imagine our
manager tasks us with writing an article about the state
of our industry. We begin to research the topic; we study
the competition, the up and comers, the trends, and
our own company's tactics. Unfortunately, the outlook
is bleak.

Industry analysts believe our organization is moving too
slowly meanwhile new players gain ground and steal
previously-held contracts. As the industry grows, the
role of our organization diminishes. In the face of this
evidence, what do we write about? If we feel fear, we
might write guile.

Fear of appearing weak motivates us to downplay the
bad news, spin it as a positive, or exclude it altogether.
Fear of bolstering our competition motivates us to ignore their gains. Fear of backlash within our company
motivates us to write a 'positive take' that disregards
purely negative indicators.

If we give into these fears, we will publish a listless
blog post that redacts vital information, assumes our
company lacks competition, and continues to pitch our
solution with a desperate and heavy hand. The result is
a forgettable compilation of words that fails to galvanize
interest. It succeeds at one thing: abating our fears.

The content inspired by fear serves the purpose of only
one person. After publishing it, the author feels safe,
feels she wrote a great piece for her company, feels she
positioned her brand carefully to avoid the invitation

of scrutiny. She is the only one left feeling satisfied; satisfied not by what she wrote, *but by what she omitted.*

Okay we get it, let's quit bludgeoning ourselves over the head with the point. But the question remains, *what do we write?* Good content is synonymous with good writing: it entertains and it educates. Good content *also* satisfies an audience of one, but the satisfaction comes from a place of pride, not fear. The author should be proud of what they present, proud to avoid self-embellishment, and proud to provide a value to readers.

This pride does not have to come at the cost of our business goals, it merely treats those goals as secondary. Our primary content goal should be to help the reader—*that's it.* If we communicate something purely helpful, we achieve our goal. Even when we discuss the myriad benefits of our product, approaching the topic from a place of helpfulness is our main priority. Let's look at some examples.

Of the three sets below, which statements represent a helpful, reader-focused approach?

Statement A
> *"We have the best tire selection in town!"*

Statement B
> *"If you love options, stop by our showroom—over 80 tire brands on display"*

In the first set, it is clear that statement A is a brag, and unless it was produced by the only tire shop in town, it's also subject to debate. Like every Tommy's burger joint that claims to be *The Original Tommy's*, this business uses an unsubstantiated superlative to lure customers.

Statement B makes no such claims and uses a fact to identify with the reader's desire for variety. This second business believes in offering a great selection, and they've communicated that to the customer while maintaining objectivity.

Statement A
> *"Fine diners with rich, discerning palates are welcome at Ariana's."*

Statement B
> *"Ariana's chef graduated at the top of her class from the world's premiere culinary school: L'école Du Chat Fantaisie[37]."*

In the second set, statement A takes the perspective of the diner, the diner that cares for a *fancy* experience. After reading the statement, someone may identify themselves with Ariana's values and discover a new favorite restaurant. Statement B achieves a similar goal, but places Ariana's needs before the customer's.

Statement A
> *"Have a question, comment, complaint, or something you want to share? Leave us a message anytime at help@ourbusiness.com."*

Statement B
> *"Customer service is important to us, we do our best to satisfy each and every comment, complaint, and request."*

The last set is trickiest; the two statements resemble each other more closely than those of previous sets. But

---

[37] Fancy Cat School.

we're getting the hang of this by now, so we've identified statement A as the reader-focused statement. While the goal of statement B is respectable, the customer goes unmentioned. The focus of statement B remains the organization and on how well it responds to customer service rather than the importance of the customer and the service requested.

If we're still a little confused as to what is meant by *good content*, we needn't fret. Throughout the course of this book we will continue to see examples of good content that helps the reader, avoids embellishment, provides value, and as a result, drives continued reader engagement, brand trust, and conversions.

Recap

'Good content' serves the customer. This service is best delivered honest and modest. But if neither of those adjectives are available, we'll settle for entertaining. Under this definition, a curated list of top Parisian museums can be just as helpful to a customer as a silly 3-panel comic about potato spuds. If our content put a smile on an otherwise unhappy face, it served that person.

Even when discussing our products, our services, or the good we do in the world, we do so while focusing on the recipient of our actions rather than ourselves. That's how we build trust, how we earn respect, and how we inspire our customers to reciprocate. That reciprocity leads to sales, repeat business, and a lasting customer relationship.

Understand Our Strategy

Time to drop the philosophizing and get to real work. To grasp what each part of this book will present, we'll first introduce our new content marketing strategy. The strategy is flexible but has a few core tenets that should remain enforced regardless of how we approach content creation. The strategy is called *Good Content*.

Figure 1

The Good Content strategy resembles a customer funnel, but one that never drops leads? (oh what wishful thinking). Our strategy acquires customers by attracting them with content related to our business (business-adjacent) that they find valuable—top-funnel content fills this portion at #1. Top-funnel content directs customers to our middle-funnel content: pieces that directly market our products and services while keeping focus on the customer and their needs (#2).

Middle-funnel content directs to other middle-funnel

content and ultimately, conversions. Upon conversion, the strategy places customers into the post-funnel content loop (#3). The pieces in this loop nurture existing customers to keep our brand on their mind, grow their relationship with us, and inspire their repeat business. That is the book's proposed strategy, the Good Content strategy, our strategy.

As we continue, we will find examples that help us generate content ideas at each point of the funnel. On occasion, the strategy seems like an overwhelming amount of work. However, a sole-proprietor can implement everything this strategy requires because it scales organically: fewer resources means fewer pieces of content, and vice-versa. But more content is not always *more* better; it's best to produce the right content, not the right amount.

In Practice

Let's assume we run a local business, a coffee shop for example (I'm a sucker for any place that puts hipsters to work). As the owners of this coffee shop, our goals are to bring customers into the store. If we're located in a major metropolitan area, Chicago for example, we begin by analyzing the search habits of local coffee shop-goers.

We stumble upon a popular search query, *top coffee shops chicago*. Looks promising. We place this Keyword[?] into our content queue. Soon we publish a piece comparing 5 of the trendiest coffee shops in Chicago. Toward the bottom, we congratulate our competition for making the list and mention how tempted we were to throw our hat in the ring (but we held back, of course).

Searchers looking for top coffee shops, would-be coffee shop goers, and even the competition stumbles across our list. The unbiased and occasionally flattering piece inspires readers to check our shop out, too (they're already on our website after all). The post leads them to a beautiful gallery of interior photographs, a menu of coffee and small-food items, and other middle-funnel content pieces.

Surprised and impressed by our honesty, the reader bookmarks our business and soon ends up at our door. At checkout, our rewards program collects their email and sends them directly to our post-funnel content loop. We take that opportunity to get feedback about our shop, coffee, and other aspects of our business to continue building a relationship with our new customer.

This is one implementation of the Good Content strategy, each business requires a tailored approach. But we can see the skeletal structure of the strategy in play: help potential customers by providing them with a value, inform them of our offering in a helpful and attractive way, then enhance their experience with our brand using post-conversion content. The last element of the strategy requires evaluating content pieces to optimize for performance. We use web analytics and customer feedback tools to determine the value of each effort. Poor performing content demands modification, and sometimes, deletion.

Is This A Lot Of Work?

If we have the capacity to release valuable pieces twice a day and evaluate our entire library's performance on a weekly basis, then more power to us. But the rule of thumb is this, *if we're not a publication, don't act like one.* Blogs, magazines, newspapers, the New York Times, these organizations are publications and with that label comes an expectation of frequency from the consumer.

However, our consumer has no such expectation of us; they expect us to deliver a service or a product, not a periodical. It is this book's opinion that our media presence should not and cannot compete with organizations dedicated to content production—that is an uphill battle easy to lose and impossible to win.

I've bared witness to billion-dollar organizations that attempted to turn their marketing teams into publishing machines. They wanted to print multiple posts a day, big stories each week, video series each month, white papers each quarter, and on until their fingernails bled. Their strategy's core focus was quantity, not quality. They fell into a trap that lures many marketers: the 7+ exposures theory.

The exposure theory purports that a prospect requires a minimum of 7 exposures to the product ('touches') before making a purchase. Frequent touches can contribute to a brand's mindshare, but the right content for the right person should generate a conversion on the first exposure, not the 87th. When we race toward high-frequency publishing goals, we sacrifice quality for quantity and we generate unnecessary and often poor content.

This strategy recommends we narrow our focus and

choose our targets wisely. We formulate top-funnel content plans that readers in our target audience will enjoy. We create middle-funnel pieces that fulfill burning questions our leads need answered. And we produce post-funnel content that builds customer relationships, not media conglomerates.

Recap

Our strategy breaks into three parts:

1. Top-Funnel content attracts new customers with helpful and entertaining content related to, but not necessarily about our business. This content directs visitors to the middle of the funnel.
2. Middle-Funnel content educates customers by answering common questions and presenting our business, services, products in a reader-centric way. This content directs users to convert.
3. Post-Funnel content provides personalized help and updates to build the relationship with the customer and lead to repeat business.

Attract New Customers

Our content strategy begins at the top of the funnel.
The top is where we focus on attracting the attention of
people who've never heard of us. Without a deliciously
inviting top layer, our content cake stays unloved and
stuck in the display case. But what belongs at the top
and how do we make it? That's what we investigate in
this first of several meaty chapters.

A Closer Look at Top-Funnel Content

We've mentioned this already and we're about to repeat ourselves, but content located at the top of the funnel *is selfless, business-adjacent, and attracts our target audience.* To break this down into its three components, we'll begin with selflessness: selfless content lacks self-promotion. Whether we wish to call it selfless, altruistic, or benevolent, this content exclusively serves the needs of one person: the reader.

When creating top-funnel content we must resist the urge to promote ourselves. When the reader arrives at our site or our video or what-have-you, they expect an answer to their concern or solution to their problem, not an advertisement. The weaving of promotional material into these content pieces takes the focus away from the reader's needs and leaves them wondering whether brand bias influenced the material. Bottom line: we don't promote at the top.

Top-funnel content is selfless.

The next pillar of top-funnel content is business-adjacency; large marketing teams shirk the idea of limiting the topics they discuss. Some content marketers will tell us that we should become a hub of all-things-related to our customer. For example, a lot of screenwriters begin, continue, and complete their work in coffee shops— I should know, I was one of them. Imagine Starbucks releases a series of how-to articles about writing your first screenplay.

In this imaginary world, Starbucks pivots their content strategy to align the needs of the screenwriter—coffee, table, free Wifi—with the needs of Starbucks: the screenwriter's money. While this strategy may drive new traffic to Starbucks' site and muster continued support for their coffee, it muddies the brand waters. Content like this begs the question, *is Starbucks focused on coffee or creative writing careers?* And the more tangents their content strategy rides, the murkier their brand focus becomes.

Top-funnel content is business-adjacent.

But producing a video how-to series or free course related to our business is not enough; what we make has to fulfill an actual desire—it must have an audience. As content marketers, we use a combination of keyword research, customer feedback, competitor analysis, and a little bit of guess-work to produce top-funnel content ideas that are likely to draw reader attention.

Attracting our target audience is the only pillar of top-funnel content that we cannot guarantee. Like every business venture, we take a risk when we produce content for the top because there's no assurance that what we produce will reach the audience we intend. For this reason we routinely evaluate the performance of our content to verify whether it finds its audience and whether that audience converts. When content does not satisfy this pillar, we modify or Prune[?] it.

Top-funnel content attracts our target audience.

We know what top-funnel content is responsible for, but how do we discover and capitalize on opportunities that satisfy that responsibility? That's the journey we begin next.

Identify Top-Funnel Content Opportunities

Regardless of what we sell or which service we provide, as business owners we require adept creative skills to succeed. Good thing, too; quality content demands creativity. With all creative efforts, there accompanies the chance to fail. I've published dozens of articles that went unnoticed, never garnering significant attention or conversions—but that's the game I've chosen to play.

As content marketers, we are in the business of making art. While our works rarely resemble the classics, we feel a connection to what we craft much like painters, sculptors, and other artists feel with their creations. As artists, this connection to our work can inspire both joy and heartbreak. When our content fails, we must try again; the top of the funnel is where our ideas take the biggest risks and reap the finest rewards.

We begin by generating ideas. We achieve this by combining business-adjacency and selflessness. We open a blank text document, spreadsheet, or good old fashioned piece of paper. Then we brainstorm a list of needs that our customer may have related to our product or service. For example, imagine a photographer who specializes in family portraits and sells prints along with her photo service. Written from the customer's perspective, her list might look like this:

- Hanging my family portrait
- Mailing my family portrait
- Printing a wallet-sized copy of my family portrait
- Preserving my family portrait
- Framing my family portrait

- Organizing all my family portraits
- Dressing for a family photo shoot
- Preparing for a family photo shoot
- Make-up, hair, and clothing choices for a family photo shoot
- Family photo shoot lighting considerations
- Taking the perfect family photo
- Arranging (blocking) for a family photo shoot
- Time requirements for family photo shoots
- Choosing the best time and date for a family photo shoot
- Who to include in a family photo shoot

The list is hardly exhaustive, but it gives us examples of how a person's needs complement her services, and vice-versa. Of course, no one person is likely to desire each need listed above, but all it takes is one. And a person's needs are not limited to pure information; needs range from entertainment to inspiration and beyond. To add more items to this list, she considers fun opportunities for content that engage visitors on a different level. The continued array resembles a series of Buzzfeed-style listicles and silliness:

- Awkward family photos
- Amazing family photos
- Family photos that didn't quite hit the mark
- Worst family photos
- Family photos past and present
- Family photos retaken throughout the years
- Disastrous family photos
- Ideas for great family photos
- Funniest holiday/Christmas/New Years cards

As she generates these lists for her business, she must do so without imposing judgment. Otherwise she may arrive at premature conclusions that belittle her ideas before they have a chance to thrive. With her initial list created, she moves to the next step in the process: attracting her target audience. To discover whether her ideas have any chance of success, she turns to keyword analysis.

Using Google's free Keyword Planner Tool[38], she can determine whether people search for the type of content she wants to create. Keyword planner provides exact figures to those with significant budgets within AdWords, but estimated keyword search Volume? is satisfactory for her purposes.

Tip

YouTube offers excellent tutorials for Google's Keyword Planner tool.

Our fictitious photographer will filter Keyword Planner's results to searches that occur near her place of business. Imagine her studio is located in Seattle; she limits her results to those within the city, within Washington state, or nearby Oregon. This filtering process removes popular nationwide trends that her local communities may not reflect. Planning family photos may be the hottest thing in Biloxi, but there's a chance that no one cares for it in Tacoma.

For this next step, she uses Keyword Planner to generate keywords for each content idea and filter the results

---

[38]https://adwords.google.com/home/tools/keyword-planner

to those that match her Intent[?]. By looking at search volume and Competition[?], she can determine whether an idea is worthy of pursuit.

Tip

Online businesses compete for a wider audience than local shops; they can stick with the broader, nationwide filter if they prefer.

For the first idea, she applies the filter and chooses the keyword, *hanging family portrait*. Keyword Planner displays over 1,000 keywords similar to the original, their respective search volumes, competition, top bids, and other data. She downloads all of it into a CSV file and imports it into a spreadsheet. She filters keyword results to those that include the word *family* and sorts by maximum monthly search volume. These are her first 10 results:

Keyword	Max search volume	Competition
family picture ideas	1,000	Low
family portrait ideas	1,000	Low
family picture wall	100	High
family photo wall ideas	100	High
ideas for hanging family photos on the wall	100	High
family photo wall	100	Medium
family photo frame ideas	100	High
family picture wall ideas	100	High

Keyword	Max search volume	Competition
family picture frame ideas	100	High
family wall decor ideas	100	High

The top two results receive at least ten times the number of searches per month than those beneath them, they do not attract ad purchases, and they happen to match one of the content ideas from her list: *Ideas for great family photos*. She makes a note of those two keywords and scans the list for others that may represent a similar Intent. In this case, she creates an Intent Group? by merging the following keywords:

- family picture ideas
- family portrait ideas
- family photo frame ideas
- family picture wall ideas
- family picture frame ideas

She combines the search volume from these 5 keywords and determines that at minimum, the demand for this Intent Group reaches up to 2,300 searches per month—searches that can lead new customers to her website.

Note

You may think that I discovered a valuable keyword opportunity first, then went back and wrote it into the book. That's far from the case.

I performed this process as described and by luck I stumbled across a popular keyword that happened to match one of my initial guesses. I write this to prove to you that the process is real and you can and will master it.

What To Create

Our photographer has discovered an idea worth her time, great! But now she has to sit down and create the thing... oh, *great*. As daunting as it seems to create something valuable out of nothing, she has a whole lot more to work with than zilch. By performing the keyword searches herself, she will form ideas for her own content based on what's readily available. When she searches for *family picture ideas*, she spots these top results:

Images for family picture ideas

→ More images for family picture ideas   Report images

100 Fun Family Photo Ideas for 2018 | Shutterfly
https://www.shutterfly.com › Ideas › Photo ▼
Aug 12, 2016 - Sweet moments always make a perfect **family photo idea**. With a simple shabby chic chair on a plain background, you can highlight the moments you love best. Shave and a haircut! For a creative **family photo idea** leave the studio behind and march your matching outfits to a fun venue like a doo-wop barbershop!

421 best Family Picture Ideas images on Pinterest | Family pictures ...
https://www.pinterest.com/thedatingdivas/family-picture-ideas/ ▼
Fun photography **ideas** for **families** including: poses, props, locations, and "what to wear" for your **photo** shoot. | See more **ideas** about **Family** pictures, **Family** portraits and **Family** posing.

116 best Family Photography Ideas images on Pinterest | Family ...
https://www.pinterest.com/janamarie76/family-photography-ideas/
Family Picture Tips & Ideas - Click for **Photo Ideas** from. **Family** Posing**Family** Pictures**Family** Portraits Posing **Families**Large **Family** Photos Fall **Family** Photos Holiday Photos**Picture Ideas**Photo Ideas. 101 **Family Picture** Tips & Ideas {The Dating Divas} Dwyer Somes - you should do a **family photo** with each of you holding the ...

Search results for family picture ideas

Our photographer notes a few elements that these top results have in common:

1. The first results are photos from Google's Image Search, so she should optimize any images she uses in her content to improve their chances of appearing in that section.
2. The titles of each result include a number: 100, 421, and 116. This encourages her to include a number in her title as well.
3. The words *photo, picture,* and *photography* are treated interchangeably—she'll need to include all three in her content.
4. Only the first link from Shutterfly is a true content piece rather than user-generated content found on a social media site; in this case, Pinterest.
5. The first result includes a year in the title: 2018. This lets searchers know that the site has recently updated the page and the page is likely to provide new information (not always the case).
6. Lastly, within the description for the first link she finds the original keyword repeated twice—note the bold phrases. The remaining descriptions look muddled by comparison.

She's seen the surface, now she needs to dig deeper. After visiting the first link she discovers that Shutterfly has not updated their post since July of 2017:

100 FUN FAMILY PHOTO IDEAS

Last Updated: Jul 7, 2017

Nothing captures the love within a family like a photograph. With the right setting, outfits and photographer, family photos become keepsakes you will cherish forever. So when it comes time to think of family photo ideas, you'll want to come up with some that showcases your family's personality.

Shutterfly's 'Updated At' line

Tip

Sites with recent content can lure would-be searchers away from established pages. Unfortunately, this site falsified their title to make the content appear newer than it actually was—as respectable brands, we don't do this.

Despite Shutterfly's *updated at* mismatch, they offer a creative piece of interactive content that allows users to filter family photo ideas:

AT HOME	SCENIC	HOLIDAY
FUN	TRADITIONAL	STAND UP	MIX IT UP
SHUFFLE	CLEAR FILTERS

For a feeling of happily ever after, capture story time in your family photo.

Photo Credit: Simply B Photos

Play a simple game like ring around the rosie to distract camera shy kids.

Photo Credit: Krissy Millar Photography

Shutterfly's Family Photo Ideas

Photographs with little text make up the bulk of the content. The filters render the piece helpful and easy to navigate. No where in the content did we find brand endorsements or links to Shutterfly's products, only photo credits. Shutterfly's business is personal photo storage and custom home decorations that make use of photographs: personalized frames, photo cubes, and others.

Knowing this, our photographer understands how individuals curious about family photo ideas make for an excellent target audience for Shutterfly. Moving on, she encounters two links to Pinterest boards. While similar in nature to Shutterfly's content, the Pinterest pages are difficult to navigate by comparison. What conclusions might she draw from these first results?

Google's algorithm aims to provide the singularly most valuable result for each search. Search engines consider the content inside the page, the number of clicks the page receives, the popularity of the page's domain, whether users conclude their search on that page, and a host of other variables when choosing which results to provide.

The top 10 results are winners, the first result being the most winner-y of the bunch. She knows that by studying the winners, she can determine what people want with a strong degree of confidence. Given that, she may conclude the following about individuals who search for *family photo ideas*:

- They want images, lots of them
- They prefer images over text
- They prefer to consume images in a grid format
- Recent updates lure them, they're looking for 'new'
- They are likely to have Pinterest accounts

As a marketer looking to build a piece of content and steal traffic away from these sites, our photographer begins planning her next moves. She will build her own Shutterfly-like page that includes a number of family photo ideas. On this page she will mix photographs she took with photographs by other photographers, asking for permission and giving due credit as she goes along.

The page provides descriptions and unique perspectives for each photograph, including potential locations and the best times of year to shoot. She incorporates the current year into the title of the page and *family photo ideas* into the description. But she's not done, there's Pinterest to take on.

She creates her own Pinterest account and collects images similar to those found in her content page—all provide valuable family photo examples, and some link back to her website. The title and description of her board also feature the year and keyword phrases. Both pieces cross-reference one another: her Pinterest board sends viewers to her site for even more ideas.

And for the searchers that come to her from the Seattle area, she creates two specific pieces of content: *30 Family Photo Ideas for Seattleites* and *43 Great Family Photo Ideas for Washingtonians*. These similar but focused pieces of content will target local searchers with precision.

By using existing customer photographs as content (with their permission), she provides both a value to visitors and a clear line-of-sight between the content and her business goals. She earns bonus points by including family photos shot by other local photographers and links to their websites as well.

To recap, here's four pieces of content she can build from this single idea:

1. **200 Creative Family Photograph Ideas for 2018**
URL: nataliestudio.com/200-family-photo-ideas
Description: Want to commemorate your loved ones with a family photo idea as unique and magical as they are? Browse over 200 family picture ideas.

2. **100+ Creative Family Photo Ideas on Pinterest**
URL: pinterest.com/nataliestudio/family-photo-ideas
Description: Commemorate your loved ones with a family photo idea as unique and magical as they are! Find over 100 family picture ideas inside.

3. **30 Family Photo Ideas for Seattleites**

URL: nataliestudio.com/family-photo-ideas-seattle
Description: It may be raining but don't worry, these 30 family photo ideas will brighten your day! Find location ideas, the best times of year to shoot, and more inside.

4. 43 Perfect Family Photo Ideas for Washingtonians
URL: nataliestudio.com/family-photo-ideas-washington
Description: Washington offers inspiring mountains, beautiful coasts, and scenic landscapes perfect for family photos. Discover amazing family photo ideas inside.

This example is everything but contrived. Our photographer used real keywords, real search results, and real content to build a sample top-funnel content plan. As a content marketer, I would vouch for and create each proposed piece listed above if working with a family photo studio. Again, this is work anyone can do, work you can do. If you feel prepared for your first exercise, move to the next section to try this process yourself.

Exercise 1

Skipping The Exercises?

If you'd like to skip this exercise for now, material continues at *Measure Top-Funnel Success*.

This exercise will task you with repeating the process detailed above. Namely, you will create hypotheses about your target audience, search for keyword evidence that supports one or more of your hypotheses, and then generate content ideas based on valuable keyword clusters. You don't have to make any of this content now; repeat this exercise as many times as necessary before you produce your first content idea.

Requirements

- Pen & paper, or text-editing software
- Access to Google Search
- Access to Google Keyword Planner[a], you must know how to:
  - Generate new keyword ideas
  - Apply filters to narrow the results
  - Export results to a CSV file
- Access to spreadsheet software that allows you to:
  - Import from a CSV file
  - Sort all rows by column

---

[a]https://adwords.google.com/home/tools/keyword-planner

Step 1: Build a List

As our fictitious photographer did, now you too must build a list of wants, desires, questions, or needs that your target audience may have in relation to your business. To illustrate, here's a few examples of what you're looking for based on real products and services:

Product or Service	Need Hypothesis
Cement mixer rental	How do I mix and pour cement?
Artisan gelato shop	Can I make gelato at home?
Fashion designer	Who are the up-and-coming fashion designers I should know about?
Private storage	What is safe/legal to put in storage?
Online shoe retailer	How can I extend the life of my shoes?

Avoid judging your hypotheses too harshly. Some portion of your guesses may not be viable... *yet*. Over time, search trends change, needs and desires change; today's lump of coal is tomorrow's diamond. With that confidence in mind, aim to build a list of **at least 25 needs, wants, or desires** before you put that pencil down or stop rapping against that old mechanical typewriter of yours.

Step 2: Guess Research

In this step, convert your hypotheses into guess keywords. Sometimes this requires no additional work, simply type the hypothesis directly into Keyword Planner's search box and hit enter. However, Google search excludes Stop Words[?] such as *I, as, how, can, of,* and hundreds more from their queries; these words appear too frequently in the English language.

When I produce keywords guesses, I strip the hypothesis down to the words that I believe Google will actually use to perform the search. Here's our hypotheses from the previous table, now accompanied by guess keywords:

Need Hypothesis	Guess Keyword
How do I mix and pour cement?	mix pour cement
Can I make gelato at home?	make gelato home
Who are the up-and-coming fashion designers I should know about?	up-and-coming fashion designers
What is safe/legal to put in storage?	safe items private storage
How can I extend the life of my shoes?	extend life shoes

With your guess keywords prepared, begin entering them into Google's Keyword Planner. Depending on your business model, you may need to apply filters at this time to narrow the results to locations where your business operates.

Tip

If Keyword Planner fails to discover keywords for your guesses, try to re-write them using different verbiage. For example, change 'up-and-coming fashion designers' to 'trendy fashion designers.'

Phrases go in-and-out of popular lexicon, so you may discover a keyword goldmine by varying your vocabulary.

Download each set of results as a CSV file. For practice, repeat this step for each keyword hypothesis you created in step 1. This may become repetitive as desires overlap and generate identical keyword ideas—don't worry about that; focus on mastering this procedure and tweaking your search terms.

Step 3: Sort Results

Using your favorite spreadsheet software, import your most promising CSV file into a spreadsheet. Remove the header generated by Keyword Planner. Sort the results by keyword volume descending such that the popular keywords appear at the top. Add a column to the sheet titled, *Intent*. Beginning with the top result, type *1* into the Intent column.

As you evaluate the second entry, ask yourself whether the keyword is analogous to the one before it. If the two keywords have a similar Intent, type *1* into the Intent column again; if their Intents differ, type *2*. Continue this process until you've assigned each keyword to an Intent identifier—this identifier groups the keywords for which Google is likely to display similar results. Earlier, our photographer collected the following keywords under a single Intent Group:

- family picture ideas
- family portrait ideas
- family photo frame ideas
- family picture wall ideas
- family picture frame ideas

After filling your Intent column, sort the sheet by Intent ascending; this organizes all of your keywords into their respective Intent Groups. By grouping the keywords visually, you can sum their search volumes to discover which groups are most popular. With everything organized, you're ready to zoom in further.

Advanced Tip

To simplify this step, use a formula to sum the volume for each Intent Group, then sort by the sum.

Step 4: Evaluate Intents

If an Intent has significant volume, that does not mean it is of significance to your business. Conversely, an Intent with little volume can help you win in a big way. This step is part art and part science as you decide which Intents are worthy of pursuing.

Begin by reading each keyword in the first group to determine whether the Intent aligns with your target audience and their needs with respect to your products. If the Intent matches one or more of your earlier hypotheses, that's great news. But don't fret if you fail to find keywords that match your guesses—that's all part of the process.

If the Intent appears valuable, scope out the average competition and cost-per-click for the Intent Group. If both the competition and cost look high, the Intent may be too difficult to win with content alone. Advertisements come before search results on Google, this leaves unpaid search results at a disadvantage. The more advertisers compete for an Intent, the less likely the searcher will scroll to organic results. But if competition is low-to-medium and cost is negligible, proceed.

Finally, perform the searches yourself to study the top results. As our photographer did earlier, evaluate the content to see what kind of results people prefer. Ask yourself the following:

Are the results what I expect?

Sometimes your keywords include branded or trade-marked terms you may be unfamiliar with. For example, people who search for *cat in the hat* are not looking for pictures of a cat, in a hat.

What formats do these results take on?

Slideshows, videos, blog posts, presentations, product pages, etc.

Can I improve upon the top three content pieces?

If you don't have the resources to create an equal or better piece of content, this Intent may prove difficult to win.

Are my competitors producing these pieces?

If so, that's a great sign that you're onto something.

If you feel confident that this Intent Group targets your audience, the expected results are business-adjacent, and the content is within your ability to produce, mark this group as a strong candidate for content creation.

Step 5: Repeat

This process will help you find top-funnel content ideas time and again. As long as people continue to use search engines to solve their problems, this exercise will enable you to meet them there.

Go to Exercise 2

If you're looking for the next exercise, skip to Inspire Conversions.

Measure Top-Funnel Success

Imagine we've written and produced a piece of top-funnel content, that's fantastic! But what comes next? The ability to measure success directly is Internet marketing's core benefit. Unlike billboards and traditional media advertisements, when users view content on the Internet they leave a trail that we can follow.

This trail includes the number of visits, where they visited from, how long they stayed, what else they looked at, and a whole host of behaviors that help us determine whether a piece of content delivers new visitors to our digital doorstep. The key metrics we look at when judging our top-funnel content are: Impressions[?], average Position[?], ranking keywords, Click-Through Rate (CTR)[?], Bounce Rate[?], New User Percentage[?], and Conversion Rate[?]. Let's look at these metrics closely.

Off-Site Metrics

Search engines collect this first set of metrics and provide them to us at no cost. To find this data on Google, we use Search Console directly or connect Search Console to Google Analytics—I prefer Search Console.

Tip

Check out the Prerequisites for links to Search Console and tutorials to help you begin using this valuable SEO tool.

From a top-funnel content perspective, our piece does well when:

- The total number of impressions is high,
- The average position is low,
- The keywords people search are those we expect,
- And the click-through rate is 5% or greater.

If our content receives few impressions, the causes vary. We may have chosen an Intent Group with limited search volume, the demand for this Intent Group may have dropped, our average position was too high, we didn't rank for the keywords we initially targeted, our content was flawed or otherwise ignored by Google, or some other penalty prevented us from succeeding.

Diagnosing this issue requires a careful study of the content, our website, and a keen eye for detail. Unfortunately, that can't be done through a book. However, we will review the most common causes of poor off-site performance and troubleshoot them right here.

Unexpected Keywords

Unfortunately, our content can rank for keywords we did not anticipate. A client of mine published a blog post that ranked for *5 stages of grief,* but by all accounts failed to satisfy that Intent. The blog post received hundreds of impressions that did not convert, and hurt the post's overall ranking as a result.

Can Solve: Remove popular keywords from our content, title, and URL that do not reflect the content within.

High Average Position

If the position of our content is too high (far below on search results) for the keywords we've targeted, searchers will never find our page. Unfortunately, sometimes the rank is beyond our control. However, we can take steps to improve our chances.

Can Solve: The content is insufficient. We should compare our content to the top results and make sure it's as high of quality, if not superior to the current winners.

Can Solve: Our domain is untrustworthy. When bad actors link to our pages, it hurts our overall reputation with search engines. We use Search Console to discover who links to us and how frequently. We must Disavow[?] any sites that look problematic.

Can Solve: The page loads too slowly. We verify this by using Google's free PageSpeed Insights Tool[?] to determine whether engines are lowering our rank due to poor site performance.

Can Solve: Mobile optimization errors. Google focuses on providing a great experience to mobile searchers as they become the source of most search queries. We use PageSpeed Insights again to see what Google thinks of our site on small screens. If necessary, we hire a web developer to optimize our site further.

Can Solve: On-page errors. Using a tool like SEOQuake[39], we can determine whether we've formatted our content poorly or lack requisite HTML elements. Errors may be so egregious that search engines ignore our pages entirely. We can hire a web developer to optimize our site for SEO.

Can Solve: Content is stale. If we published a piece more than a year or two ago, we've provided competitors an opportunity to win with recent content. We solve this by updating our content with new information and changing the title to reflect the update.

Can Solve: Keyword overuse. Using SEOQuake or a similar tool, we can determine whether our content is over-

---

[39]https://www.seoquake.com/index.html

saturated with target keywords. The practice of keyword over-saturation is known as Keyword Stuffing[?] and receives a ranking penalty from search engines.

We solve this by reducing keyword repetition to a maximum of 3% of all text. Focus on using keywords in the title, headers, and first paragraphs.

Cannot Solve: Too much competition. When domains with more clout than our own publish great pieces that break the top 10, smaller businesses struggle to compete.

Low Click-Through Rate

If our content ranks for the keywords we targeted and receives a good number of impressions, a low CTR renders that success moot. If users don't click on us, it doesn't matter if we're in the top 10. Thankfully, a low CTR is often the result of some common issues.

Can Solve: The page's Title[?] fails to entice users. Sometimes a title is incapable of catching the searcher's eye, but by updating it we may better lure a would-be clicker. Experiment with the title to attract more attention.

Can Solve: The Description is weak or unrelated. If we fail to set a description for the page or we've written one that trails off and lacks our target keywords, searchers may skip right past our result to one with a better hook. Rewrite the description and limit this text to 160 characters.

Can't Solve: Too many ads. If our competitors begin to pay for placement on these keywords, we will lose the attention of searchers. We can't keep our competition from buying ads, but we can purchase our own if we know that our content converts well enough to warrant the spending.

Low Impression Count

This isn't always a problem; sometimes we target keywords with low traffic because they represent highly-specific Intents (otherwise known as Long-Tail Keywords?) and bring the perfect customers to our site.

However, if we intentionally targeted high-traffic keywords, we can fix some obvious causes of low impression counts.

Can Solve: Keyword mismatch. If our content does not include the keywords we intended to rank for, then search engines will never place us on the right result pages. We fix this by editing our content to include the target keywords (and variations thereof) that do not exceed 3% of the written words. We can also edit our title and URL to better represent our keywords.

(Probably) Cannot Solve: The keywords are no longer popular. Sometimes interest wanes and our content loses relevance. There is one potential solution: discover new keywords that act as synonyms for our original Intent Group. We then edit our content to reflect this change in trends and lexicon.

On-Site Metrics

We must collect this second batch of metrics on our site and through our analytics setup. By default, Google Analytics tracks the bounce rate and new-user information already. To track conversion rate (or Page Value?), we must take the extra step to establish goals within Google Analytics.

Tip

Find both paid and free Google Analytics resources among this book's prerequisites.

A piece of top-funnel content performs well on-site when:

- The bounce rate is low, or notably lower than site average,
- The percentage of new users arriving at our content is higher than site average,
- And the conversion rate is 5% or higher.
  - If tracking page value, we aim for higher than site average.

If our top-funnel content exceeds among these three metrics, it's doing its job: attracting new visitors who stay on our site and ultimately convert. However, not all of our content will perform well right out of the gate. Here are some common causes of poor on-site metrics and suggestions on how we might improve our chances.

High Bounce Rate

A bounce rate of 90% or higher indicates that users leave our website as soon as they're finished with our top-funnel content piece; but we want them to stay. Remember, top-funnel content introduces our brand to new customers; if they bolt as soon as they meet us we'll never get a chance to deepen our relationship with them.

Can Solve: First load slowness. The first time we visit a website, we download all the images, assets, HTML, code, and the fixins' that run the site. But on subsequent visits, that data is stored by our browser and the page loads much faster. Therefore on average, first visits are slow.

If our new users spend 10 seconds or less on our content, they may be leaving due to impatience. We can use Google's PageSpeed Insights tool to discover what is slowing our site or more specifically, our content page. We can hire a developer to optimize our website and improve load times.

Can Solve: No where to go. If we forget to link to relevant pages within our site, the user may finish our content and have nothing to do but leave. We fix this by improving our navigational elements, e.g. about us, home page link, contact link, and others that are found on all pages—and looking for perfect linking opportunities within the content itself.

If the content can send the reader to another top-funnel piece or an ideal middle-funnel page, we're more likely to keep them on the site and move them along their conversion path.

Tip
Readers are likely to click-through to another page *after* they finish the content. Visitors who make it to the end are better primed for the 'next thing;' therefore links toward the bottom of our content have a better chance of receiving a click.

Low New User Percentage
When the majority of users arriving at our top-funnel

content have been to our site before, it could mean two things: the content is such a big success that users can't help but visit repeatedly, or the content has lost popularity in search.

Can Solve: Content has lost organic popularity. We need to go back to the off-site metrics and look for improvements there. If we can improve impressions, CTRs, and keywords, we will raise our new user percentage.

Low Conversion Rate

Something is amiss if visitors land on our site, browse around, and never convert. A lot of factors play into the conversion rate, but some are likely to impact the results. Let's take a look at a few obvious causes that render our top-funnel content conversion-less.

Can Solve: Irrelevant content. Perhaps the piece is not as business-adjacent as we'd hoped. We may be serving the content to the wrong crowd or targeting a segment of users that cannot access our products or services. To fix this, we reconsider whether the content aligns with our business goals.

Can Solve: Poor tone. If this is the only piece of content that struggles to convert, we should compare the writing to that of more successful pieces on our site. Perhaps this one is too pushy, not helpful enough, or otherwise leaves a bad first impression.

Can Solve: Low volume. If the content receives a relatively small share of all the web traffic coming to our domain, then of course it will fail to lead to significant conversion rates. In this case, we need to boost our metrics on search to see an increase in volume.

Can Solve: Poor links. If the content succeeds in attracting hundreds or even thousands of visitors, perhaps it sends them off to the wrong place. If the content links to less than a handful of pages, we should look to them as likely culprits. We then fix this by improving those pages or swapping for better links.

Cannot Solve: Factors beyond content. If the goal we're tracking struggles to convert regardless of where the user comes from, content cannot help us there. We need to go back and reconsider our goal, how we track it, and other particulars beyond the scope of this text.

Recap

Let's review what we've learned about metrics. At a high-level, a piece of top-funnel content performs well when:

- Impressions received are **high**,
- Average position held is **low**,
- Keywords for which it ranks are those we targeted,
- Click-through rates are **5% or greater**,
- Bounce rates are **notably lower** than site average,
- Percentage of new users acquired are **higher** than site average,
- and the conversion rate is **at or above** site average.

Ideally, we evaluate these metrics at monthly intervals to determine the rate of growth (or decline) of our content. Search trends are seasonal, so it's best to overlook the day-to-day numbers and focus on how the content performs in the long run.

It takes time to gather a trusted Internet following, so we must avoid beating ourselves up if we're not raking in thousands of visitors on day one.

To easily recover these metrics (and more) in a single spreadsheet, I recommend URL Profiler[a].

---

[a]http://urlprofiler.com/

Refresh and Re-Purpose Top-Funnel Content

An insignificant, almost non-existent sliver of Internet content is both timeless and requires little, if any update. This is known as 'evergreen' content. Occasionally we create a piece of evergreen ourselves, but human nature demands us to worship at the altar of the new. We want new stimulus, new ideas, new puppy gifs to look at.

After we publish an amazing piece over which we sweat and bled, an invisible countdown clock begins to tick. This clock counts down toward irrelevance day, the moment our content turns stale and begins to lose traffic. Our content can avoid this fate in one of two ways: **refresh** or **re-purpose**.

Refresh Content

At about the one-year mark, a thorough and high-quality piece of content may begin to lose its luster. Consider the fate of a top 10 list, a product review, or an Instagram photo of Kim Kardashian, they all lose value in time. After a year, we have more options to consider for our top 10. After a year, the product's manufacturing process or design may have changed. After a year, Kim gets a new haircut so that 'gram is hella old.

? Do kids still say, 'hella'? Did they ever say it? Please advise.

But by refreshing a piece of content we can avoid the clock-hands of fate. Depending on the topic of the original piece, sometimes refreshing requires a few small additions, a title change to reflect the update, and an Indexing? request made of the search engine. That may be all that is required to get back into the top rankings.

However, if a lot has changed in the arena of our topic, a small adjustment will fail to satiate our readers. We may have to research the piece all over again and perform edits that impact a large portion of the work. But this work is valuable: a winning piece of content should not suffer the fate of time. If we put in the effort, the content should continue to deliver new users and valuable business for years to come.

Re-Purpose Content

If we have nothing new to investigate within our topic and a refresh fails to boost the rankings, we may consider re-purposing successful content instead. To re-purpose is to serve the same content in a new way. As a consultant, I wrote a 5-piece series for my client that we later re-purposed into a Slideshare page (a LinkedIn product), a condensed article written for a new audience, a YouTube presentation, and a live conference talk. Each time, I made slight modifications to the original content. This strategy can inspire new interest in old topics and find audiences beyond the search engine.

While creating new content is fun and exciting, re-purposing is easier because it recycles existing knowledge and pulls from content that has already won. And by re-purposing content, we explore new channels that may deliver a new audience.

When All Else Fails

"If you want to increase your success rate, double your failure rate."

– Thomas J. Watson, Former Chairman and CEO of IBM

No matter how hard we try or how long we persevere, some content never delivers—that's okay. At the top of this chapter we agreed that content is in fact art. As art, content may fail to find an audience and fail to bring success to its creator. That's doubly okay. We do not start this journey expecting every thread we spin to turn to gold.

If we go through the entire top-funnel content process and our piece has earned us few conversions, little traffic, and is otherwise dead-on-arrival, we must prune it. Pruning requires us to remove the content from our website, remove links to that content, Deindex? the content from search engines, and redirect users to somewhere valuable.

We must be careful to follow a specific order when performing these steps, otherwise readers may find themselves on our 404 page.

1. **Deindex the page from search engines.** We ask Search Console to remove a specific URL from our site property. This removes it from search results temporarily (90 days), but we still need to take the added step that removes the page from our hosted content.
    - If we have images in the content, we need to request their removal as well. Each image has

a unique URL that we must submit to Search Console's URL remover tool.

- We perform this step for each search engine from which we receive visits: Bing, Ask, and potentially others.

2. **Redirect users to another page.** We must employ a 301 Redirect? to send users to a page that converts better than the original content. Often we redirect them to our homepage.

    - We can perform this task within CMS tools, like Squarespace and WordPress.

3. **Remove all links.** We find all pages on our site containing a link using the following Google search query: site:oursite.com link:oursite.com/link-to-find. We edit these pages to remove all references to the content.

4. **Delete the content.** In this last step, we remove the page from our site permanently. Bye-bye content, long live the content.

The Top-Funnel Content Process

We've covered all the stages of our top-funnel content strategy in this chapter; it was a lot. To avoid skimming back and forth through this section, use the following as reference for the full top-funnel strategy, the strategy that attracts new customers to your business.

1. **Ideate**

Perform Exercise 1 to discover new content ideas, build keyword hypotheses, research them for validation, and merge them into Intent Groups.

2. **Create**

Choose a valuable Intent Group and create a piece of content that targets this group. Remember that content is not limited to blog posts; content takes the form of white papers, case studies, video series, infographics, quizzes, podcasts, and so much more.

3. **Publish**

Publish and promote the content. This process requires notifying search engines of new pages on our website, sharing to relevant social media channels, and broadcasting to fellow businesses (if included in the content).

4. **Measure**

In one month's time, we study both on and off-site analytics collected for the content piece. We measure impressions, clicks, bounce rate, conversion rate and more. We take appropriate action to correct or improve any lackluster metrics.

5. **Refresh & Re-Purpose**

In a year's time, we look at our metric trend lines to see whether the interest in our content has waned. If the content grew stagnant, we refresh and re-purpose the content to inspire new interest.

6. **Prune**

Lastly, if the content fails to draw significant attention or lead to meaningful conversions, we remove it from our website and deindex the piece from search engines.

But enough about what customers want. It's time to talk about what *we* want: money!

Inspire Conversions

Just kidding about that money part. However, we have arrived at the chapter which helps us create content strictly focused on one thing: ourselves. Our content strategy is incomplete if we fail to speak to our strengths, our purpose, and our value. But remember when we discussed how writing from an *us-perspective* rather than from the customer's perspective can inspire mistrust and come off as boastful?

By focusing on the reader's point-of-view, we avoid that arrogant blunder. But simply writing from the customer's perspective is not enough to earn their business. How do we convince readers of our value without shoving it down their throats?

Make Them Feel It

During my study of the English language and literary writing, I came across an exceptional piece of advice that overlaps into the copy and content world: do not tell readers how to feel; feelings must be felt by the reader. Consider the following passages:

Passage A
Hoping for no sign of her pursuer, Bridget nervously peeked around the alley corner: there he stood.

Passage B
Back pressed to the wall, Bridget's trembling fingers inched her shaking body toward the alley entrance. Perhaps at last she outran her pursuer; five deep breaths would still her. Hoping to find no trace of his towering figure, she peeked one weary eye around the corner: there he stood.

These passages exaggerate the point, but there's a valuable difference between the first and the second. The first passage narrates a feeling, it dictates it. By doing so, it has asked the reader to define what nervous means in this situation. Our minds were tasked with creating the atmosphere of 'nervous,' a process that originated at the feeling, nervous in this case, and terminated at the side-effects.

We may have imagined Bridget's back pressed to the wall, her body trembling, or her soul ruffled, but we did not experience nervousness. The second passage provided the side-effects and tasked us with interpreting their source. Passage B did the hard work of creating a nervous atmosphere and gave us the opportunity to connect to the text and feel it for ourselves. But how does this apply to writing about our products and services?

To find out, let's take a look at two more passages. This time we're going to look at a slogan, but not just any slogan, but a reimagining of the world's most iconic:

Passage A
Feel exhilarated as you overcome your own inhibitions and lack of motivation. Imagine how successful you will be after completing that morning jog, that 5k, that marathon, that run across America. You are going to feel so good.

Passage B
Just do it.

Combined with beautiful images of athletes pushing their bodies to new limits, Nike's slogan cuts to the emotional core of those who hear and read it. Three words create an atmosphere because they connect to an audience that sacrifices an extra hour of sleep every morning. That audience feels the lure of a warm bed calling them back, of an extra hour of amazing television, of a crazy night out with friends.

Nike reminds them that those three words can push past temptation and toward athletic glory. I feel it as I write this and as I read the slogan again; rather than telling me what to feel, I imagine the situation in which I use these words and they inspire the corresponding feelings within me.

Using this strategy, we can write about ourselves in a way that inspires our audience to feel great about our products and services. For a simple example, let's consider an electronic kettle. If you've never used one before, an electronic kettle boils water without an open flame. One merely flips a switch and the water within comes to a boil shortly thereafter—simple enough.

Now let's imagine the team at Kettle Co. has worked tirelessly to design a kettle that never spills: the *Kettle IV*. Their design handles accidental drops without spreading boiling hot water all over the place. But the team struggles with how best to relate this new feature to prospective kettle customers. They have three options to consider:

Option 1

> *Our triple-layer design and lock-valve prevents boiling water from escaping the kettle during accidents. Kettle Co.'s patented technology makes Kettle IV the safest electronic kettle on the market today.*

The first option is written from an 'us' perspective. Pronouns like *our* and *we* litter the copy and place the emphasis on what the business has achieved rather than what it can provide to its customers. That kind of bragging may attract their ad segments, but it stinks up their content and copy with *Parfum du Sales Tactics*.

Option 2

> *As their heating elements activate, kettles become a dangerous liability—you and your family deserve to feel safe in your kitchen. Introducing the Kettle IV, a spill-proof kettle that will never burn you or your loved ones.*

The second option does a better job of placing the focus on Kettle Co.'s customer. The passage informs family-oriented kettle owners that their current kettles are not as safe as they may think. The primary issue with the second passage lies in its visualization. The passage dictates the value directly to the reader: *this kettle will never burn you.* While that gets the point across, it does so without inspiring the emotions Kettle Co. wants to associate with its product.

Option 3

> *Every parent has a no-no list. Toxic cleaning products? No-no. Lawnmower? No-no. The boiling hot water kettle? Definitely a no-no. But supervising your kids all day is not an option, meanwhile everything you forbid draws them in like a siren's song. That's why unattended kettles send 340 children to the emergency room every year.[40] You've done your best to provide a safe home for your kids, now it's our turn.*

> *At Kettle Co. we believe that boiling water should be a risk-free experience for all families. That's why we designed the first kettle that never spills: the Kettle IV. Finally, you can cross 'hot water kettle' off the no-no list—but lawnmower? That one's not going anywhere.*

Option 3 takes a significantly different approach by building a visual for the reader. Cleaning products, whirring lawnmowers, and boiling hot water readily draw upon the fears every parent experiences. The statistic pushes this fear further into reality, the reality of owning an electronic water kettle as a parent.

But option 3 refuses to leave the reader frightened. The passage quickly segues into feelings of empowerment

---

[40]Fake news, please remain calm.

(*you do your best...*) and of having support (*...it's our turn*). The product is what provides the support by preventing burns, but the passage leaves the reader responsible for making that connection. By mentioning *never spill* rather than *never burn*, the passage inspires images of a boiling kettle knocked over by a child. The hot liquid in the kettle, confined, the innocent child, unharmed. Those images and the feelings associated sell the kettle, not the features.

When we combine strong visualizations with a costumer-focused approach, we are free to discuss the benefits of our products and services without sounding pushy or dry.

Recap

At the core of great copy lies great writing. But to go beyond capturing the imagination of our target audience, we focus on their perspective and the benefits they receive. Customer-focused writing helps readers imagine themselves buying our products, recruiting our services, and doing business with us.

When we combine wholesome marketing with excellent products and tremendous customer service, we create a triple-threat weakness-free business.

For writing help, remember to check out the Prerequisite section for my all-time favorite writing resources. But as a shortcut, we refer to this table when writing about ourselves and our business:

Do

- Write from the customer's perspective.
- Help the customer visualize themselves using our products and services.
- Tell stories and paint pictures with words.

Don't

- Make it all about us.
- Tell them how our products and services will make them feel.
- Torture them with humorless or otherwise dry material.

Identify Middle-Funnel Content Opportunities

Unlike top-funnel content that requires research and significant guess-work, discovering middle-of-the-funnel opportunities is straight-forward. As business owners and content leaders we have a substantial understanding of the value we offer to customers (or at least we pretend to).

We can take this value and break it down into features, services, use-cases, and more; that's the easy part. The challenge comes in choosing which of the ideas we should produce, if any. For an example, let's revisit our photographer friend in Seattle.

As a family photographer she shoots weddings, family portraits, baby showers, Bar Mitzvahs; we name it, she photographs it. Naturally, a number of these fall under a single category: family events. Alternatively, our photographer may choose to further break each service down to its own dedicated page. By the end of her brainstorm, the proposed Sitemap[?] may look like this:

- **Home Page**
  - **Services: Photography** A top-level page that talks a little bit about our photographer's history in Seattle, photography in general, what it's like to shoot with her, how she wants customers to feel about their photos.
    * **Family Portraits** Shows off beautiful family photos and tells the stories of several satisfied clients. This page offers a CTA[?] to

call, email, or send the studio address to their mobile device or email.

* **Family Events** Tells the story of capturing great family moments that can never be repeated. It goes on to help customers imagine what it's like to look back on their favorite times with friends and loved ones.

  · **Weddings** Dedicated to weddings and littered with beautiful brides, dressing room shots, the kiss, the line-ups, engagement photos, everything.

  · **Precious Moments** Misfits section that offers a service for everything else. A war veteran's return from overseas, a baby's first steps, an artistic photo series, a holiday celebration, and more.

  · **Coming of Age** Devoted to Quinceañeras, Bar and Bat Mitzvahs, and other cultural celebrations of the transition to adulthood. Collections may include collages from early childhood to the event itself and unique framing opportunities that capture that growth.

  · **Baby Showers** Special treatment shown for mothers-to-be and all the antics that take place when surrounded by friends, family, and Mimosas.

– **Services: Printing and Framing** The photographer goes into detail about sharing the customer's photographs with loved ones, seeing special moments every day at home, and paying homage to beautiful events with appropriate framing and positioning.

  * **Printing** While respecting the customer's option to take their digital copies anywhere,

it honestly portrays the range of canvas
and fidelity options provided by the photographer and the resulting quality of each.
* **Framing** It begins with the utmost deca-
dent, hand-carved frames and ends with
simple black matte that goes with any dé-
cor. The photographer offers wrap-around
options and discusses the pros and cons of
each frame.

This looks like *a lot*, I hear you worry to yourself. Generating middle-funnel content ideas is terribly simple,
but knowing which to follow-through on is the true
challenge. In our photographer's case, the bevy of content she must now create to serve her myriad use-cases
overwhelms her. She paces back and forth, scratches
her head, wonders if any of it is necessary or perhaps
if all of it is. Let's give her a chill-pill by introducing a
new piece of information: *when planning middle-funnel
content, start with nothing.*

Yes, nothing. If we don't have a website, then we're already ahead of the game. Writing an entire sitemap full
of middle-funnel content puts the cart before the horse;
we are not the drivers of our middle-funnel strategy, the
customers are. Let's return to the photographer. To start
with nothing means the shutterbug creates a simple
home page that provides her name, logo, address, phone
number, email, and a brief list of services—essentially a
simplified About Page.

The photographer's top-funnel content pieces link to
this homepage whenever she highlights a professional
service. Given the right context, visitors understand that
the link they clicked on, e.g. *capture beautiful wedding*

moments, represents a service offered by the photographer.

As her top-funnel content grows in popularity and brings new traffic to her site, she invariably faces questions from prospective customers. Questions will come in on the phone, through email, in letters, in person, and via cuddly carrier bunnies (cutest option). The questions posed to her will form the skeleton of her middle-funnel content strategy.

She knows this well in advance and prepares by tracking each and every question in a spreadsheet. She takes note of how often she receives each question and evaluates the set at the end of each month. If she can answer the question in a paragraph or less, for example, *what's your cancellation policy*, she solidifies her answer in writing and includes it within an FAQ page.

However, if a question is broad, requires examples, existing customer input, or proves rather opinionated, she considers building a piece of middle-funnel content to satisfy that thirst for knowledge. For example, three dozen customers may ask her, *how do you shoot weddings?*

Weary of repeating herself for the umpteenth time, our photographer crafts a top-level Weddings page that showcases gorgeous photographs, customer testimonials, and copy that focuses on that special day and what she's willing to do to make it perfect for the bride and groom. In it she answers every sub-question that falls under the same umbrella: *will you travel for wedding shoots, do you include an engagement shoot, how far in advance can we book you*, etc.

Why this strategy? Let's remember that all content we create exists to serve the customer—even content that's meant to sell. We set out on a strategy that gives us every chance to help, not every chance to lecture people about our greatness and accomplishments. Yes, writing about our achievements and what we're capable of feels rewarding and leaves us with a sense of pride—save it for the memoir.

When it comes to content, prospective customers trust us when we focus on them and deliver the information they desire. The alternative leaves them wondering, *gee, they sure do love talking about themselves.*

Exercise 2

Skipping The Exercises?

If you'd like to skip this exercise for now, material continues at *Measure Middle-Funnel Success*.

We learned that the simplest middle-funnel content strategy involves placing the customer front-and-center by stripping our middle-funnel to nothing but a home page and waiting for questions to arrive. But what if we have an existing business with an existing website and very-existing customers? This exercise will help us establish a question-tracking spreadsheet, identify unnecessary middle-funnel content pieces on our site, and help us generate new ideas based on existing customer concerns.

Requirements

- Access to your sitemap and/or website structure
- Access to your web analytics tool
- Access to spreadsheet software
- Customers creeping over your shoulder (optional)

Step 1: Gather Questions

If your ear finds itself close to the ground, you may have a beat on the common questions posed by your customers. If so, open up a brand new spreadsheet and write each down. If you haven't the faintest clue as to what your customers ask—perhaps you're too high up the ladder, *hello from below!*—then pull your front-line employees aside for a few minutes to pick their brains. By the end of step 1, you should have a healthy list of questions that your customers ask over and over again.

Step 2: Identify Existing Content

If you have a website and have yet to itemize your content pieces into a spreadsheet, you will do that now. Otherwise, you may skip this step. To qualify as a middle-funnel content piece, it must speak of your business, products, services, or features exclusively. If you've written top-funnel content that begins to discuss your business, that content does not belong on this list.

Consequently, this step may take you some time if you have a large web property. Thankfully once you've completed this step, a little maintenance is all it takes to keep your content spreadsheet up-to-date. At minimum, you should track the title, URL, and questions answered by each page—you will complete that part in the next step.

Beyond that, here are some valuable fields worth tracking in this spreadsheet: description, page value, conversion rate, % of all sessions the page participated in, date last updated, and others we'll cover in *Measure Middle-Funnel Success.*

Step 3: Evaluate Existing Content

Now that you have a complete set of your middle-funnel content, you're ready to compare it to the questions list. As you evaluate each piece of content, follow this guide:

- If the content answers a question from the list, mark the content as *May Require Improvement*
- If the content fails to answer any question from the list, mark the content for *Pruning*

Step 4: Prune

If a piece of content fails to answer even a single customer's burning question, prune it. Leave any pieces that have an above-average Page Value, conversion rate, or similar.

Step 5: Improve

Why might your content need improvement? Naturally if your middle-funnel pieces answered the questions to each customer's satisfaction, fewer customers would ask those questions. There are several possible causes for this discrepancy:

1. The content is difficult to reach (few links to the page, page not found in top-level navigation)
2. The answer lies obscured by a larger topic
3. Customers are unaware of your website
4. Customers are not searching for answers online

Reason № 4 will continue to diminish until 2049, the year in which the percentage of living organisms with broadband beamed directly into their skulls will approach 100. But in all seriousness, there's not much you can do to resolve № 4 on your own. If the likely cause is № 3, investigate how customers discover your business and whether you can meet them there with appropriate content.

More readily solvable are causes № 1 and 2. If your site provides valuable information that is buried under a poor menu structure or worse, Adobe Flash?, then you can improve its visibility. Add relevant links to the page, rename the page, and place it within top-level navigation. Remember, this is a burning question your customers need an answer for, don't be shy when providing them access.

Finally, if the answer to the question is a paragraph trapped in an essay, shine light on the info. If the parent content runs long, add a table of contents at the top that lets readers drop directly on the anchor point where the answer lies. Alternatively, give the answer a brand new page and prominent placement in the top-level navigation menu.

Step 6: Answer The Unanswered

Source your middle-funnel content proposal list from any remaining unanswered questions. Remember, if the answer is objective, e.g. *What are your hours*, then a placement within an FAQ or About Page is sufficient. However if the question is open-ended, requires your opinion as a content creator, or demands a long nuanced dissertation, the question earns a solo piece.

Sometimes you have the opportunity to group multiple questions (both subjective and objective) into one piece of content. In the case of the photographer, imagine she receives the following three questions more frequently than all others:

- How far are you willing to travel for wedding shoots? (Objective but long)
- How long in advance must we book you for our wedding? (Objective)
- What packages do you recommend for a winter wedding? (Subjective)

Creating an individual piece of content for each question will prove unnecessary and leave each piece feeling incomplete. Does she really need a page for *Destination Wedding Shoots* and one for *Booking in Advance* and yet another for *Winter Wedding Packages*? No. It is clear that each of these customers will gravitate toward a *Weddings* page.

A single page can provide a table of contents that leads readers directly to the answers they seek. Answering related questions in a single middle-funnel content piece reduces your mental overhead and the number of pages a reader must navigate before finding their answer.

Brainstorm a list of content additions you would like to make to your site:

- Top-level pages that answer one or more related questions
- FAQs that provide quick answers to objective questions
- Existing pages that can benefit from an update or additional content

Step 7: Repeat

After pruning, old customer questions may begin to resurface—that is expected. Your site answered them at one point, but no longer does. This forces customers to ask these questions anew and for you to find placement for their answers among your middle-funnel content pieces.

This may prove an awkward process but one that helps you discover and track historical customer queries as well as those that crop up over time. As new questions appear, repeat this process and look for opportunities to fold new answers into existing content or create brand new pieces that show off the incredible work you do.

Go to Exercise 3

If you're looking for the next exercise, skip to Reduce Churn.

Measure Middle-Funnel Success

Measuring the value of top-funnel content is straight-forward: simply answer, *are people showing up to my site?* But middle-funnel content has a different goal: it must inform the customer of our business and effectively sell our services. But we direct organic traffic to our top-funnel content pieces, not our middle-funnel. New users are unlikely to land on our middle-funnel pieces and therefore the conversion rates for these pages is poor—that's expected. Then by what metric do we measure the success of middle-funnel content? Enter Page Value.

To quote the glossary:

> *"Google Analytics calculates a page's Page Value by summing its contributions to both revenue and goals, then dividing by the number of unique visitors that page received."*

By tracking each page's Page Value, we can discover which pages play a significant role in our conversion funnel. Middle-funnel pieces are naturally found in the middle of the conversion path as top-funnel content leads users to them, and they in turn lead users to product pages, checkout pages, and contact us forms (depending on our online business goals).

If our business sells products online, then our Ecommerce transactions will distribute page value naturally along the conversion funnel. But if our online goals are limited to directing visitors to sign up for a newsletter or fill out a contact form, those actions lack inherent monetary value. To calculate page value without an

Ecommerce site, we assign dollar values to our goals. But what is a goal worth?

We calculate the value of a goal by discovering the average Customer Lifetime value[?] (CLV) of all individuals that completed the goal. This requires that we have LTV data and that we can segment customers into two groups: those that completed the goal and those that did not. If we don't have this information, the next best bet is to assign each goal an identical value, $100 for example.

This second approach will not provide an estimate of each page's contribution to our bottom-line, but it offers a measuring stick that compares the value of one page to another. Neither approach proves entirely accurate, but by assigning a value to our goals we discover which middle-funnel pieces bring visitors closer to conversion, and which leave them wanting more.

But page value is not our only measuring tool; let's look at Drop-Off Rate[?]. This metric tracks the percentage of users that abandon a conversion flow at a given page. The drop-off rate is similar to the bounce rate; but where the bounce rate applies exclusively to Landing Pages[?] (pages at which the user begins their session), drop-off rates apply to all pages along the funnel.

Google Analytics defines conversion paths for us by studying our traffic, but we can generate custom paths that identify a series of pages we expect the user to navigate before arriving at a goal. For example, we might define a path for each top-funnel content piece that resembles the following:

Top-funnel piece ->
  Link to middle-funnel 1 ->
    Link to middle-funnel 2 ->

Link to Contact Page ->
Contact Us Goal

Google Analytics tracks the percentage of users that abandon both user-defined and automatically-generated content pipelines; our middle-funnel content makes up the bulk of these pipelines. By looking at the Behavior Flow report, we can discover which pieces of middle-funnel content excel at spurring our visitors toward their conversions and which send them off to the wrong direction, or worse, off to another website.

Our middle-funnel content performs well when:

- The page value is higher than site average,
- And the drop-off rate is lower than site average.

When faced with fledgling middle-funnel content pieces, we have a few solutions that may troubleshoot ineffective pages.

Lower Than Average Page Value

When the average page outperforms middle-funnel content, something is amiss. Remember that our funnel in fact assumes a cone shape beginning with a mass of top-funnel content that narrows to a small number of middle-funnel pieces and ultimately down to conversion. Therefore, the majority of conversions go through middle-funnel pieces. If one of these pieces has a low page value, we may be able to troubleshoot the cause.

Can Solve: Unlinked and unloved. Perhaps a recent change has removed or broken links from our top-funnel content to our middle-funnel piece. Use the Google search trick,

link:oursite.com/to-the-middle-funnel-piece
site:oursite.com

to discover all pages that link to our unloved middle-funnel piece. If the link count is low, we should look for opportunities to link it up.

Can Solve: Fails to inspire conversions. If the content lacks punch or lacks links to pages where conversions take place, then the piece won't play a significant role in converting customers. We can fix this by improving the content and adding a call-to-action at the bottom.

High Drop-Off Rate

When readers abandon our flows at our middle-funnel pieces, then our pieces are failing to connect with them. We keep in mind that they clicked on the link and arrived at the piece, but something sent them astray. Here are common causes that send users elsewhere.

Can Solve: Irrelevant links. If we link to places we don't want visitors to go, we shouldn't be surprised when they go there. For example, readers do not have the same altruistic expectations of middle-funnel content pieces as they do top-funnel: we don't have to advertise alternatives to our services when discussing... our services.

To solve this, we remove unnecessary links that send users out of our conversion path and off our domain.

Can Solve: Top-to-middle disconnect. In our top-funnel pieces, we sometimes oversell when we link to our middle-funnel content. For example, *the best flowers in the world* sets up high expectations for readers who follow that link. If they arrive at our middle-funnel piece and find their expectations unmet, they may leave due to disappointment.

Alternatively, a major middle-funnel content update may render our link text inaccurate. To correct this, we look for all links that brings top-funnel readers to our updated middle-funnel piece and correct them for any inaccuracies or distasteful exaggerations.

Advanced Tip

When searching for links to a page using,
"link:oursite.com/link-to-page",
we can exclude results from our domain by adding,
"-site:oursite.com."

Can Solve: High Latency[?]. Just like top-funnel pieces, middle-funnel content can also suffer due to long load times. This is the case when top-funnel content exists on another website or platform. If a popular article on Medium.com sends readers to a middle-funnel piece on our site, that middle-funnel piece acts as a landing page and therefore, the reader's first exposure to our domain.

To fix this, we follow the same procedures described in *Measure Top-Funnel Success*. Namely, we correct for a high bounce rate.

When All Else Fails

When we try our hardest to no effect, what then? Compared to poor top-funnel content that we simply prune and forget about, middle-funnel work answers questions vital to our customers and business—we can't just drop it. When our middle-funnel pieces fail despite loading quickly, possessing meaningful links, and providing answers in a captivating way, we have to turn to someone for help.

One thing this book cannot do is remove the pair of rose-colored glasses writers don when reviewing their own work. Put simply, sometimes we believe our work is fantastic, but we're alone in our beliefs. Turning to a trusted colleague or friend can help us see past our clouded judgment to the truth: our content might suck.

As a consultant working for a tech company led by optimistic employees, I witnessed plenty of over-confidence. Occasionally, the pieces my client produced were laden with superlatives and grandiose claims— they loved what they wrote about themselves. Meanwhile, I saw their writing as chest-pounding that frequently failed to help the customer.

Together we worked to 'tone down the rhetoric' and focus on delivering value. By bringing a 3rd party into the mix, one that feels at liberty to disagree with our approach, we can discover issues hidden beyond our perspective.

Recap

We've discovered that middle-funnel content does
well when:

- The page value is **above average**,
- And the drop-off rate is **low**.

Much like their top-funnel cousins, we evaluate
middle-funnel content once per month to track performance over time. To do so, we can import the
metrics by hand into the same spreadsheet we use
to track each of our middle-funnel pieces.

We can pull page value, drop-off rate, session count,
and more into a single sheet that identifies each
row by two values: URL and date measured. We can
filter results to a single page and chart its progress
month-over-month.

Alternatively, we can use Google Analytics to build
a custom report for our middle-funnel pages and
use the Compare Date feature. However, Google Analytics limits historical data collection to 25 months;
keeping a copy elsewhere permits additional year-
over-year comparisons.

The Middle-Funnel Content Process

Creating and maintaining middle-funnel content is less about research and trends than it is about our customers and their needs. Middle-funnel content exists to provide answers in a way that connects with our audience and sells our products. As a reference, we may consult the following table of middle-funnel process stages when creating, maintaining, evaluating, and pruning middle-funnel pieces.

1. Initial Pruning

Performed once for an existing website, we boil all middle-funnel content down to a single homepage that summarizes objective information: e.g. name, logo, location, hours of operation, phone number, email or contact form. We remove all but the highest-performing middle-funnel content pieces.

Initially, all top-funnel content will direct to our homepage nexus (unless targeting specific product pages for an online store).

2. Question Mining

As part of a continuous process, we gather customer questions and collect them in a spreadsheet. If we work beyond the front-lines of our business, we glean this information from peers and subordinates.

3. Evaluation

We evaluate our existing middle-funnel content pieces as they relate to customer's requests:

- Do we need to create new content to answer customer questions?

- Do we need to shine a light on existing pieces of content?
- Can we group multiple objective and subjective answers under a single piece?
- Should we repair the tone and focus of a previously us-centric piece?

4. Creation

We build the required content pieces or edit existing content to include new answers. For objective questions, we write objective but warm responses. For subjective questions, we paint pictures for our target audience that leaves them feeling positively about the experiences we can deliver.

5. Measurement

We correct for high drop-off rates and low page values as best we can. Middle-funnel pieces that continue to suffer despite our best efforts may require pruning, restructuring, or a review from an impartial editor.

If we do great middle-funnel work, our content begins to convert visitors into customers as we sit back, relax, and rake in all that revenue. Then it's time to close the book, forget about those silly customers, and take a permanent vacation to Opposite Town.

Reduce Churn

Already back from vacation? So soon???

"Depending on which study you believe, and what industry you're in, acquiring a new customer is anywhere from five to 25 times more expensive than retaining an existing one."

– Amy Gallo, Harvard Business Review

The third and final section of our book involves Churn[?], a piece of jargon whose origins I dare not investigate. Perhaps due to feckless reading habits, the word churn sometimes reminds me of a pile of rotting fish. But the churn we're discussing is the rate at which customers disengage with our business: the pace at which they stop buying from our stores, cancel their subscriptions, or otherwise abandon our services.

What gives? To list every possible reason a customer may desert a business would require more time than we have on this Earth. However, great post-funnel content can help prevent some common causes of churn, namely:

- **Lack of Engagement**
  Our business ceases to communicate with the customer in a meaningful way.
- **Poor Documentation**
  We fail to provide content that helps customers enjoy our products.

- **Regrettable First-Time User Experiences** (FTUE)
  Content that introduces new customers to our business, products, and services provides a poor initial exposure, or none at all.

Post-funnel content has the unique responsibility of maintaining a strong relationship with existing customers. By producing and distributing post-funnel content, we increase the likelihood that our customers continue to engage with our business. And when we combine post-funnel content with other relationship marketing efforts, we increase customer retention. Here's what the Harvard Business Review had to say on the topic:

*"If you're not convinced that retaining customers is so valuable, consider research done by Frederick Reichheld of Bain & Company [...] that shows **increasing customer retention rates by 5% increases profits by 25% to 95%.**"*

Define Post-Funnel Content

Compared to the previous content funnel stages, the definition of post-funnel content is a bit more nebulous. This content varies sharply from business to business, and therefore its purpose and format remains difficult to prescribe. However, by looking at copious examples we will discover opportunities to create post-funnel content for our products and services. If we had to define it, we would say that post-funnel content is any such work that improves the customer's experience.

But without familiarity with this funnel stage, it is challenging to distinguish post-funnel content from the previous two stages. Yet post-funnel content has one key distinction from the rest: it speaks to a *sold* audience. For readers who've already bought into our value, a piece of middle-funnel content often features unnecessary fluff.

Post-funnel content may speak more directly to what our customers desire in a warm, objective tone without the need to paint pictures. And whereas top-funnel content must address popular desires to remain successful, post-funnel content need only address our customers, not the engine-surfing masses. But like all content we produce, post-funnel should remain customer-focused and helpful, it must do good.

Note

Occasionally, we serve middle-funnel content to existing customers when we introduce new products, features, or services to them—whenever we up-sell.

Otherwise, we serve existing customers with post-funnel content.

Identify Post-Funnel Content Opportunities

As stated earlier, the form and purpose of post-funnel pieces remains unique to each business. To help us generate ideas, let's look at three businesses distinct in their size, target audience, and industry: our local Seattle photographer, a chain of mid-western burger restaurants, and a business that belongs to America's most hated industry—shh, it's a surprise. Let's start with whom we're most familiar with: our shutterbug.

As a reminder to us all, she sells photo packages, touch-ups, prints, custom frames, and other services related to photography. Before we go into direct examples, let's ask ourselves, *what might inspire customers to engage with and continue their relationship with this photographer?* Here's what we came up with and the formats in which our photographer would deliver them:

Blog Posts and/or Short Emails

- *Tips on Hanging Your Family Portrait*
- *How to Clean Prints Without Damaging Them*
- *What to Write on Your Holiday Card*
- *Did You Know Prints Fade Over Time? Learn How to Preserve Them*

Short Emails, Letters, and/or Postcards

- A seasonal reminder to send holiday cards
- 1-year anniversary 'time-hop' to each client's previous photographs
  e.g. "Re-live Your Beautiful Wedding (in Photos)!"[41]

---

[41] Before firing this one off, she should check to make sure the client is still married.

The average monthly ad budget pales in comparison to the cost of a single stamp. Sometimes the thoughtfulness of a personal post-funnel piece can turn a one-time customer into a lifelong fan. This approach scales well for a service-oriented business with a measurable client base, but what about a business that serves hundreds or thousands of anonymous customers per day?

Enter the burger chain. Generating post-funnel content ideas is difficult when we focus on a business that sells consumable goods. Once the product is consumed, it's *out of sight, out of mind.* What can post-funnel content do to challenge that timeless idiom? Here's what we came up with:

- **Burger Tracker Kit**
  A laminated take-home menu sheet, a fridge magnet to hold it, and a dry-erase marker. This menu beautifully displays each burger adjacent a checkbox.

  Customers track which burgers they've already had and can leave little notes about each. Staff present first-time customers with a kit and their first burger already checked off. And the restaurant offers each customer a burger on-the-house in exchange for a completed tracker.

  The menu also acts as a brand reminder and quick reference for phone number, location, and hours of operation.
- **Kids Coloring Book**
  Restaurants already provide children with drawing utensils to keep them distracted, why not continue the artwork at home?

  Seasonal coloring kits (with accompanying crayons)

can provide children the opportunity to color and our business to leave subtle reminders to parents.

- **Nutrition Recap**

Most adults know perfectly well that burgers are not the healthiest meal available. Wouldn't it be great to discover that the restaurant we chose actually took steps to insure our burger was as healthy as possible?

This pamphlet, email, or blog post digs into the ingredients found in the customer's burger, the source of each, how the restaurant stored them, and the methods used to prepare them. All for well-being of the customer.

The content can also include suggestions for additional healthy options upon the customer's return: lettuce wrap, baked fries, and other healthy hot-swaps.

- **Staff Trading Cards**

This one is a bit weird, which is why we like it. Imagine each staff member has a baseball-style trading card that depicts them in a funny photo, offers a small bio, and shares their favorite burger and how they order it.

Customers receive a random one after dining at the restaurant and earn a free meal after collecting 10 unique cards. Trades encouraged.

An inverse relationship exists between the brevity of customer-to-business interaction and the creativity required to produce valuable post-funnel content for that customer. If our relationship to the customer is purely transactional, we have to work extra hard to generate post-funnel opportunities that serve customers well.

That is why in this previous example we have explored gift-giving. Offering a gift, especially when personalized, can engender the customer's desire to reciprocate. Again, a seemingly small personal gesture can lead to large relationship gains and repeat business.

Okay, we've looked at post-funnel opportunities for products that people love: photographs and food. But let's attempt to build a relationship with customers of the most hated industry in America. According to the American Customer Satisfaction Index®, the industry that proved least satisfactory among American consumers in 2017 was our beloved Internet service providers.

Time Warner, Xfinity, AT&T, Charter, and other familiar names all made the list. But imagine they experienced market pressure that required them to remain competitive; what kind of post-funnel content could they provide to build a better relationship with their customers?

Note

It's difficult, if not impossible to imagine a positive relationship between customer and ISP. So please suspend your disbelief for the next few minutes.

Here's what we came up with:

- ***Where Does Your Bill Go?***
  A Blog Post, Email, Pamphlet, or Landing Page that breaks down how the ISP spends customer money. If honest, this can help reveal to customers that their ISP isn't such an evil money-grubbing-oligarch after all.

For example, the ISP may detail what percentage goes to paying employees, operational costs, profit, charitable donations, infrastructure investments, and other categories.

- *Safe Surfing: A Guide to Encrypted and Unfettered Access to the Web*
Counter to the mission of ISPs that collect usage data and sell it to 3rd parties, this ISP helps its customers hide their online behavior by dissecting private browsing, HTTP vs HTTPS, virtual private networks (VPNs), and the Tor browser in a Blog Post, technical document, or landing page.

- *Meet Your Customer Service Rep (CSR)*
According to the survey, poor customer service significantly impacted the industry's overall score. So instead of an automated system that connected customer requests to unknown call center employees, the company introduces customers to their CSR beforehand.

  With a Pamphlet or Leaflet sent to them along with their first bill, the ISP can provide a brief introduction to the CSR which includes their name, direct line of contact, a short biography, and other personal details to help connect and humanize the estranged parties long before their first of many shouting matches.

- **Rate Increase Warning**
This comes in the form of an email or letter that warns customers of their forthcoming promotional rate expiration. ISPs generally offer 12-month rate discounts to entice customers to sign up, but rarely do they warn customers when the promotion is due to expire.

  In a warm and sincere tone, the content may provide alternatives to customers who find the new rate unaffordable. For example, the content may present lower-tier plans that the customer can afford without seeing an increase in their bill. Better yet, the content offers them a way to lower their bill even further.

It is possible even for a business as vilified as an ISP to find little victories with post-funnel content. I personally hope you're not in the ISP business, but if so, feel free to steal these ideas—especially if you work for Xfinity and run marketing for the Midwest's 100 Mbps plan. Just saying...

Recap

Post-funnel content opportunities can take many forms but they all strive to achieve the following goals:

- Help the customer (do good)
- Up-sell if and only if the customer will benefit
- Improve the customer's product/service experience

Armed with these goals in mind, we can identify post-funnel content without the pressure to deliver new leads to our site or convert them to paying customers.

Post-funnel is about fun and friendship, about joy and partnerships, about a tugboat made of ice cream on a river of rainbows. Mmm, ice cream.

Exercise 3

Skipping The Exercises?

If you'd like to skip this exercise for now, material continues at *Measure Post-Funnel Success*.

Hopefully by now we've seen enough examples of post-funnel content that we're able to get an idea of what works and what doesn't. So now it's your turn, dear reader, to come up with your own. In this four-step exercise you will source ideas from a variety of creative springs. Grab a pen and paper, or yet another spread-sheet, and get cracking.

Requirements

- Access to results from exercises 1 and 2
- Access to sitemap or webpage structure
- Access to pen / paper, spreadsheet, or document editing software

Step 1: Dig Through The Top Rejects

In exercise 1, you generated between a handful to dozens of top-funnel content hypotheses that simply didn't pan out. Perhaps the keywords weren't there, volume was dismally low, or competition insurmountably high. What-ever the reason, you have leftover scrap ideas that may yet see the light of day if you drag them into the post-funnel world. Ask yourself the following when evaluating your rejected ideas:

1. *Can I tweak this idea to better target my existing customers?*
2. *Will this content improve my customer's experience as it relates to my business?*

Copy down all ideas that pass the test; these are great candidates for post-funnel pieces because they help readers and you've already vetted them for business-adjacency.

Note

Do not confuse post-funnel with top-funnel content. Despite their similarity in tone and helpfulness, top-funnel content should remain optimized to attract and convert visitors into customers with appropriate linking.

Meanwhile, post-funnel should remain optimized to nurture customer relationships. Linking to middle-funnel content within post-funnel is bad form—existing customers who've bought into our value will wonder, *why are you still selling me?*

To reduce confusion, sequester top-funnel and post-funnel blog posts into separate categories when possible. An argument can also be made to exclusively limit blog posts to post-funnel content (paying customers are likelier subscribers to our blog, anyway).

Step 2: De-Salesify The Middle

Are you loving the titles for these? In step 2, you will look through all of your existing and planned middle-funnel content for recyclable material. Large sites have numerous middle-funnel content pieces; your job is to scan through your middle-funnel for work that you can tweak into ready-made post-funnel. As you glean over each middle-funnel piece, ask yourself the following:

- *Assuming my customer has never read this, will a matter-of-fact version improve their experience as it relates to my business?*

Often times the answer is *no*. If customers have already bought in, there's little they can learn from middle-funnel marketing pieces because the information contained within is likely past its *Use By* date. But for an example that works, let's imagine that a top concern of potential ISP customers happens to be, *how do I install the modem myself?* The ISP went through the trouble of creating a beautiful landing page that shows off how quickly customers can get their modems up and running without technical support. Fantastic.

But ISPs often acquire customers exposed to little or none of their marketing (because consumer options for ISPs usually number in the low ones). In the case where a customer signs up and chooses to install the modem themselves, a how-to guide recycled from the landing page is a great piece of post-funnel to offer this user. By stripping out the imagery and call-to-action, this middle-funnel piece can become a valuable post-funnel guidebook that improves the customer experience.

Step 3: Let's Get Physical

The Internet is a great place to acquire customers but it's not always the best place to help existing ones. Depending on your business, people currently enjoying your products or services have likely taken them offline—they're using them in the real world.

Newsletters can absolutely bring them back online, but those emails often go unopened and rarely provide the timely experience-boost that post-funnel content brings. Whether your business exists entirely online, otherwise, or somewhere in between, put on your brainstorming cap and start to list ways you can help your customer in the real world.

In earlier examples, we saw the following physical post-funnel items:

- A postcard that acts as a seasonal reminder to snap and send holiday cards
- A postcard that acts as an anniversary 'time-hop' to a previous photo shoot
- A seasonal children's coloring book
- A magnetized burger tracking kit to help customers record which burgers they've tried
- Collectible staff cards, baseball-style
- Letters or pamphlets that introduce ISP customers to their CSR, encrypted browsing, and more

Unlike digital content, printing and distributing physical goods often comes with additional overhead. Order your ideas by feasibility and take a stab at the expected costs you may incur by implementing them. Obviously, you don't need to commit to any of these ideas right now and you'll learn why in *Measure Post-Funnel Success*.

Step 4: Update 'Em

Where's the fun in this title? Oh, I think this is where I stopped paying my editor. This last step has you collect the changes, features, and improvements you've added to your business over the past year. As you list the changes you've made, check whether existing customers can or have benefited from these modifications.

Whether customers already receive this benefit or whether they must perform an action before securing its effects, plan to create and publish content that tells them about it (if you haven't already done so). This is perfect blog post and short email material.

Measure Post-Funnel Success

This section will explore the unfortunate reality of post-funnel content, mainly the fact that measuring its success requires math and a lot of guess work. Due to the variety of formats post-funnel content can take and its lack of quantifiable outcomes, measuring its value requires us to wrap ourselves up in lab coats and run some experiments.

By experimenting, we mean performing literal experiments with beakers, lightning, and Igor, our creepy hump-backed assistant. But an experiment may be overkill for the occasional post-funnel blog or snail-mail post card. However, if we plan to create physical content that requires a significant investment, we should run an experiment before deciding to fully commit to the expensive strategy.

Experiment with Real-World Content

Note

Experimentation is time-consuming and expensive work. We do not perform experiments of this magnitude unless the post-funnel requires similar levels of commitment. For one-offs or strictly online post-funnel pieces, skip to the next section.

Post-funnel content aims to improve the customer's experience, but is 'experience' a quantifiable variable? No. But we can measure the byproducts of great post-funnel content, namely the customer's satisfaction (tracked via survey) and their Customer Lifetime Value (CLV). If we don't already track CLV for each customer, we must do so before performing our first experiment. We can calculate a historic CLV using the following generic equation:

$$CLV = (T * AOV) * AGM * ALT$$

Attribute	Definition
T	Average monthly transactions
AOV	Average order value
AGM	Average gross margin
ALT	Average customer lifespan in months

If we track and acquire these data points, we can proceed with the experiment. If we already calculate CLV as well, that's great because our version is likely better-suited to our industry than the generic model above. With that prepared, we can begin.

To perform the experiment, we begin to assign new customers to one of two groups at random: **A** and **B**. We place 90% of new customers into group **A**, the group that remains unexposed to our new post-funnel content, otherwise known as the control group. The remaining 10%, group **B** receives the post-funnel content. The total of customers we place into the experiment are known as the cohort. When the cohort reaches a significant sample size (10% of annual customers is a good target), we stop adding customers to the experiment and we wait...

And keep waiting...

The amount of time we must wait differs based on industry, business, and products sold—we use our best judgment before gathering results. Once we've waited long enough, we can administer the surveys. To best control the experiment, we send the survey to both groups simultaneously; this helps account for seasonality and other effects brought on by time.

As the survey results roll in, we begin to compare group **A** to **B**. Depending on the questions asked in the survey, this may require math and some manual labor, e.g. reading comments and averaging scores. We also track meta metrics like the average number of days before receiving a response and the response rate of both groups.

Finally, we compare the average CLV of both **A** and **B**. If group **B** clearly expresses a superior experience with our business and achieves a higher average CLV than group **A**, those are strong signals that we should continue to invest in this post-funnel strategy.

> **Tip**
>
> For easy and free survey software, look to Google Forms[a]. For more professional survey options, consider Survey Anyplace[b] or Typeform[c].
>
> ---
> [a]https://www.google.com/forms/about/
> [b]https://surveyanyplace.com/
> [c]https://www.typeform.com/

Track Happiness

When we publish post-funnel content online or in email, we can gather customer reactions on the spot by incorporating in-line feedback tools. While imperfect, these tools survey the customers as they consume our content. For examples of this in practice, we look to customer service emails that solicit feedback below the CSR's reply a la, *was this response helpful?*

Often accompanied by large *Yes*, *Maybe*, and *No* buttons, clicking one sends customers to a page that lets them complete a survey. On individual pieces of web content, we can solicit similar feedback with questions like, *was this article helpful?* The drawbacks to this approach are several:

- Survey responses may not correlate strongly with the customer's future behavior
- Some surveys are administered at relevant, but biased moments
  - A single piece of content may upset the customer temporarily, but leave their long-term satisfaction unaffected, or vice-versa
- When gathering feedback anonymously, we're unable to associate the feedback to a specific customer, and in turn, a specific CLV
- If our customers rarely appear online, we may not gather a sufficient number of data points

However, the general satisfaction of customers correlates with our post-funnel efforts. While engaging customers with content is not the only way to satisfy them, content can have a marked impact. A well-executed piece of post-funnel content can be the difference between receiving a grateful testimonial or an angry customer service call.

To track the effect of post-funnel, we begin monitoring customer satisfaction (if we don't already) and observe the trends over time. If providing post-funnel content has never been our focus, we will see a measurable growth in customer satisfaction after distributing great post-funnel pieces.

Tip

To gather customer feedback, consider Opinion-Lab[a], Kampyle[b], Hively[c], or similar tools.

[a]https://www.opinionlab.com/
[b]http://www.kampyle.com/
[c]http://teamhively.com/

When To Send Newsletters

Never.

This book's strategy puts us through the workload ringer: research, spreadsheets, top-funnel, middle-funnel, post-funnel, voodoo rituals, it's enough to spin an exorcised head all the way around. Twice. But when we sit down to look at all the work ahead of us, at least we can cross *newsletter* off of our list.

Like tickle-me Elmo, gluten-free diets, and bangs, newsletters are a fad. If our customer's inbox is a jar of sweets, the growing collection of neglected candy corn settling at the bottom is a trash heap of newsletters. Newsletters fester because many of the businesses that create them prioritize cadence of delivery over customer needs.

Marketing teams wrongfully assume that frequency will win the day; they push to publish content regardless of what their customers want. But let's ask ourselves, when scores of our customers contract salmonella at our restaurant chain, will they feel reassured knowing that we served raw chicken the same time every week? No, but newsletters remain big business—why?

It's in the name: businesses that benefit from producing *newsletters* happen to produce *the news*. When content is our product, curating a newsletter comprised of our 'product' and sending it off to customers is a great way to engage them. Businesses that do so include publications, bloggers, social media celebrities, and others. But *content as a business* is different than *content as marketing*. We're here to market, not become another overnight blogging billionaire success story (those don't exist).

That covers what *not to do* and saves us a boatload of stress and labor. Yet this section exists and it therefore must serve a positive purpose.

Newslesser

See what we did there? Better email marketing strategies exist than the incessant beat of a dull newsletter drum. Rather than shooting off 8000 over-stylized
emails every two weeks filled with background noise,
we can segment our customers and send them personalized plain-text emails at favorable times. Here's why
those attributes matter:

- **Personalized**
  Traditional newsletters are over-produced and rarely,
  if ever do they take the recipient's desires into account. Newsletters are also time-consuming to create. Crafting multiple and segmenting customers
  into newsletter funnels is an unpopular burden
  that most content producers refuse to take on.
  By choosing to personalize, we send fewer emails
  and simplify the content within.
- **Plain-Text**
  By plain-text we mean an email that looks like it
  was written by a friend or colleague. No fancy borders, big corporate logos, or high-res stock images.
  Those elements are perfect for teasing a new product release, but they're awful for building customer
  relationships.
  The over-produced content begs the customer to
  conclude, "they didn't go through all this trouble just for me." And the truth is, *we sure as hell
  didn't.* We sent that million-dollar email to everyone we've ever met—and their dogs.
- **Favorable Times**
  Favorable for the customer, not the business. Delivering a newsletter every Friday at 5 PM may be
  favorable for the content team, but the customer

doesn't care about the content team and their deadlines, now does she?

However, after she receives prints of her family photos, that's a perfect time for our Seattle photographer to send her a follow-up email that asks for feedback on the prints and offers an article as well, *Tips on Hanging Your Family Portrait*. Ba-da-boom.

Example

Subject: Ready to hang those photos, Alex?

Message: Hi Alex,

According to the tracking info, your prints arrived today! I hope they're everything you wanted (and that we *perfectly* captured your beautiful family).

Please let me know if you have any issues with the photos you received, I will straighten problems out for you immediately.

Best,
Natalie

Natalie's Photo Studio
123 Lane St
Seattle, WA
1-123-456-7890
nataliesphotostudio.com[a]

P.S. If you need any help hanging your photographs, check out *Tips on Hanging Your Family Portrait*[b].

---
[a]

[b]

By keeping emails personal, plain-text, and delivered at times convenient to the customer, we significantly increase the chance that customers open our emails, respond to us, and engage with the post-funnel content within. This hand-crafted process may sound like more work than the mass-produced newsletter, though in reality we can use those same email marketing tools to segment customers and deliver personalized email. But we'll spend more time crafting tailored communications, and less time tinkering with templates or forging useless articles.

> **Tip**
>
> For personalized email marketing, this book recommends Gmelius[a] for small customer bases (requires a Gmail account) and Drip[b] for larger customer pools.
>
> ---
> [a]https://gmelius.io
> [b]https://www.drip.com/

What Now?

You've finished this brief but (hopefully) enlightening text, you may be asking yourself, *what do I do now?* If you haven't already, go through the exercises in order. If you've performed the exercises, run them again because now you're armed with the bigger picture. After completing the book, you understand how all three elements of this strategy work together to build leads, conversions, and trust:

Top-funnel ->
  Middle-funnel ->
    Conversion ->
      Post-funnel ->
        Conversion ->
          Post-funnel ->
          ...

If you are starting your web presence from scratch, then your immediate next steps are:

1. Build a homepage that defines the purpose of your business and provides objective data: name, logo, email, hours of operation, phone number, and other relevant information. Nothing else.
2. Integrate Search Console and Google Analytics into your website.
3. Define at least one goal (conversion) in Google Analytics. For example, *Submit Contact Form*.
4. Create a piece of top-funnel content based on results from Exercise 1.

5. Publish and link your top-funnel content to your homepage.
6. Measure response to top-funnel, adjust content as necessary.
7. Use customer questions to create or update an FAQ or other middle-funnel content.
8. Reassign top-funnel links to more appropriate middle-funnel pages, if applicable.
9. As customers arrive: plan, create, and publish post-funnel content for them.
10. Track CLV and customer satisfaction, adjust post-funnel as necessary.
11. Repeat steps 4-10.

If you run or belong to an established business, the steps you take from here depend directly on where your business stands. The factors that come into play are size of the business, attitudes toward content and self-promotion, current state of content, resources you may allocate to content creation, structure of the website, and others. This book can't prescribe the right path for you, but the following questions may help you get started:

- **Is this strategy one you agree with?**
  If not, you may want to consider looking into other strategies, such as the one famously promoted by HubSpot[42].
  If you do agree with the strategy's premise, what are the first 5 steps you can take to get a Good Content strategy rolling?

---

[42]https://blog.hubspot.com/insiders/content-marketing-plan-success

- **Is your organization prepared to take the risks required of this strategy?**
  Risks include: treating your competitors with respect (even when they don't deserve it), being honest about your flaws, and showing vulnerability. Implementing Good Content requires flying in the face of what many consider industry best practices and common sense.
  If your organization is unprepared to follow the strategy, what might you do to win them over?
- **Are you prepared to learn the requisite skills (or hire someone who already possesses them)?**
  Without an analytics tool, access to search results, and proper feedback gathering mechanisms in place, implementing this strategy is next-to-impossible; it relies on data.
  What small step can you take to begin learning these skills? Can your organization afford to hire someone who possesses them or pay you to learn?
- **Are you prepared to research, write, edit, and publishing content?**
  This book's strategy does not put you or your team on a content schedule (thank goodness) but it still demands a lot of work.
  If you're not prepared to tackle it all, what tiny bit of effort can you exert to get the ball rolling?

Kernels of Wisdom

Great business books (doubtless this is an instant classic) often leave readers with bits of incredible advice buried in thousands of words—not this one. As a committed reader of this book, I award you with a printable two-pager that summarizes the Good Content strategy and key tips to act as a reminder of everything you've learned (or already knew). This document acts as a quick reference point for whenever you need a bit of guidance but can't quite reach the book nor the exact spot in the book where I buried those tiny bits of wisdom.

Download the printable PDF[43]

or scan the following QR code from a mobile device:

Scan this QR code to download the PDF to your mobile device

Please keep in mind that this PDF remains unpublished for exclusive access to readers, to you. Share it with no

---

[43]https://storage.googleapis.com/good-content/good-content-two-pager.pdf

one, *or else.* Just kidding! You can share it with anyone just as long as they sign an oath...in blood. No biggie.

Bonus: A Surprise

If you paid close enough attention, you realized halfway through that this entire book is a piece of top-funnel marketing—a pretty large one. And like all top-funnel marketing, this book is completely free. Wait, you paid money for this? Oh wow, awkward. I apologize for *this obvious mistake* and swear it will never happen again (so much winking right now). I know just how to make it up to you.

This book provided you with everything you need to build a successful content strategy for your business. However, if you would like help creating your content, implementing the strategy, modifying your website, incorporating third-party tools, or improving your return-on-content-investment, then consider scheduling a meeting with me.

If you choose to work with me, you will receive 15% off the ticket price for our first project...*and* whatever you paid for this book. To contact me, use the following email:

contact@stanleyidesis.com

and mention this book's unique coupon code: *how-dare-you-make-me-pay-for-this*. Or you can schedule a meeting with me right now[44] by clicking that link, directing your browser to http://bit.ly/good-content-consultation[45], or scanning the following QR code:

---

[44]https://calendly.com/stanley-idesis/good-content-consultation
[45]http://bit.ly/good-content-consultation

Scan this QR code to schedule a meeting from your tablet or smart-phone

One Last (Meta) Thing

Now that you know this entire book is part of my content strategy, I want to give you a peek behind the curtain to show you how I used my own strategy in this book:

- You may have noticed that I used 'we' and 'us' when not speaking directly to you, the reader. I did so to engender feelings of inclusion. You, as in *us*, are content marketers. I wanted to write from a voice that did not talk at you, but with you.
- To inspire your trust, I included alternatives to services that I also provide. I readily admit that I'm not the only option for you and this book is not the only strategy out there. (It's just the #1 Best Original Tommy's Strategy, *obviously*).
- I waited until the very end to pitch myself. Readers who made it this far were more likely to consider my proposition and remain focused on the content (what they came for) rather than thinking I wrote the book merely to peddle myself.
- And lastly, I chose to include the aside you're reading right now. I'm taking a risk by doing so, by showing my hand, by being vulnerable, by opening myself up to criticism.

Feel free to steal these tactics, they're in your hands now, *literally*.

You've reached the end of the book! If you are ready to try the exercises (or would like to try them again), begin at Exercise 1.

Glossary

#

42   According to some nerds, the *meaning of life.*

A

Adobe Flash

The devil; so much so that Adobe themselves want to cast it back to the hell from whence it came. Adobe will end support for the aging technology in 2020, for good this time. If our website relies on Flash, we must remove it and replace it.

Two factors drive content creators away from Flash: poor performance and the inability of search engines to access Flash content. By trapping content within Flash, no search engine is capable of determining what we've nested inside—that's bad. Flash is a no-no.

B

Black Hat

Black hat encompasses any SEO optimization tactic that attempts to game the ranking system. Black hat techniques include keyword stuffing, hiring link networks, building a network of fake sites to point to ours, and others.

This book recommends we ignore black hat techniques in favor of straight-forward value creation and honest networking.

Bounce Rate

The percentage of sessions for a single page that ended without navigating to another page or performing any tracked action. Essentially, if a user arrives on one of our pages then leaves, or if they leave the page open for 30 minutes, they count as a bounce and increase the page's bounce rate.

A high bounce rate is generally unfavorable.

C

Call-to-Action (CTA)

Our call-to-action is the one behavior we want our visitor to perform after they enter our funnel. Depending on our business, a CTA may be: sign up for our newsletter, contact us, make a purchase, subscribe to the service, start a free trial, leave a comment, download gated content, etc.

CTAs are most commonly found on landing pages within middle-funnel content.

Churn

The rate at which customers unsubscribe from our services or cease purchasing our products at expected intervals. The exact calculation varies between businesses, but a monthly subscription service churns a customer when that customer cancels their subscription. That type of churn is easy to calculate.

However, a company like PG&E may struggle to determine whether a specific customer has stopped purchasing their laundry detergent. A restauranteur may not notice the missing regular. Churn like this happens all the time; reducing churn is a top priority for all businesses.

Click-Through Rate (CTR)

We calculate a page's CTR by dividing the number of clicks it received by the number of impressions it received over a given time span. For a search result with an average position of 1, a CTR of 25% is expected.

Competition (AdWords)

AdWords represents keyword competition by a value ranging from 0 to 1. The closer competition is to 1, the more advertisers vie for ad placement on the keyword. A high competition value means that organic results likely suffer from limited impressions due to the series of ads that dominate the top of the results page.

Users click on ads, and ads are the first "results" they see. The more ads there are, the less likely searchers are to scroll past them in search of organic listings.

Content Management System (CMS)

WordPress, Squarespace, and similar site-building tools are a type of content management system. Traditionally, CMS tools stored and provided developers access to a website's content, e.g. images, text, products, blog posts.

But in recent years, the purpose of CMS tools has broadened to include hosting complete websites.

Conversion Rate

The number of sessions that include a conversion divided by the total number of sessions. To contribute to a single page's conversion rate, users begin their session on that page and ultimately complete a Goal or make a purchase.

Note that conversions need not occur on the page itself, but the page must act as an entry point which ultimately leads to a conversion.

Comma-Separated Values (or CSV File)

A CSV file is a primitive text file that organizes data into rows and columns. The first line establishes the header, and every subsequent line represents a row in the table. When possible, we export data to CSV and then import the CSV into our favorite spreadsheet software.

By exporting data to CSV, we can share the data with people that have limited access to the original tool or who use alternative spreadsheet software.

Customer Lifetime Value (CLV)

A CLV attempts to calculate the profit a given customer brings to our business. The CLV can be historic and therefore based solely on existing data or it can be speculative. Speculative CLVs act as our best guess as to the total business the customer will bring over the course of our relationship with them.

The formula for calculating CLV varies among businesses, but the historic average CLV is calculated by summing the transactions for all customers and dividing by the total number of customers. We may calculate a speculative, and therefore more useful CLV, by multiplying average transaction value by average monthly transactions, average gross margin, and average customer lifespan (in months).

However, the most accurate CLV for each business requires tweaking to take their unique customer patterns into account.

D

Deindex

The deindexing process removes a URL from search results. If the URL can already be found on Google or Bing, we must use their respective tools to remove the page: Google's Removal Tool[46] and Bing's Removal Tool[47]. Deindexing is a necessary step when pruning our content.

Description (or Meta Description Tag)

Provided by a page's `<meta name="description">` tag, the description offers little impact to ranking but gives us a second opportunity to entice the searcher to click on our result.

The description should paraphrase our content, appeal to the reader, and repeat our target keywords (all in 160 characters or less). Search engines place in **bold** words or phrases in our description that match terms found in the user's search.

If using a CMS like WordPress or Squarespace, the tool provides direct access to this important data element.

Disavow

Our domain's reputation impacts the search rank-

---

[46]https://www.google.com/webmasters/tools/removals
[47]https://www.bing.com/webmaster/tools/content-removal

ing of all pages found on our domain. When domain's with a poor or toxic reputation link to ours, their reputation comes with them; this hurts our reputation in turn.

We can perform a disavow operation on webmaster tools to prohibit these links from affecting our rankings; it's kind of like *un-friending* a website. To perform this action, we navigate to the Disavow tool provided by Search Console, Bing Webmaster, and others. The operation must be completed for each search engine.

Drop-Off Rate

A page's drop-off rate indicates the percentage of sessions that end on that page without a conversion. The lower the drop-off rate, the better the page serves the customer and sends them along to the next step in our funnel.

G

Goal (Google Analytics)

Visitors can achieve goals that we establish for our Google Analytics properties. Goals are highly flexible and can be the result of: events triggered on a page, time spent on a session, a number of sessions reached by a user, an item purchased, and more.

By establishing meaningful goals, we gain a better understanding of which pages and users contribute most to our success. Goal examples include: signing up for a newsletter, reaching a checkout page, commenting on a blog post, and more.

H

HTML5

The latest accepted standard in website document markup. HTML5 brought with it a slew of improvements over standard HTML, and all major browsers support the new standard.

I

Impression

An impression is defined as a single user seeing our search result a single time. For example, when a user searches for, *banana bread* and sees a list of 6 websites on their screen (before scrolling), each of these sites receive a single impression.

Indexing

A web crawler (or bot's) job. Indexing is the act a crawler performs as it finds new pages on the Internet. When it comes across a new page, the crawler adds it to the search engine's index.

For example, Google's index keeps a record of many active (and some inactive) pages thanks to the indexing process. And when we "Google something," we don't search the entire Internet, we search the content available on Google's index.

This is why some search engine results can remain out-of-date with the actual content on the page or why they occasionally point to pages that no longer exist (the bots haven't gone back there yet).

Intent

The human desire behind a keyword search. When

we're incapable of articulating our desires directly, we often write out our intent using keywords. For example, imagine a searcher trying to find a picture of a Narwhal. However, they only recall the animal's appearance, not its name; so they type this into the search box: *sea animal like a dolphin but with a horn.*

While that keyword does not include Narwhal even a single time, Google properly returns webpages dedicated to Narwhals; the search engine understood the Intent behind the keyword.

Intent Group

An Intent Group is a collection of keywords whose Intents are similar, but not identical. For example, the searches *silly cats* and *funny cats* have different human intentions but can likely be satisfied by the same result.

A page of funny cat photos is an arguably formidable solution to the desperate desire for kittens of both searchers.

J

JavaScript

The programming language that, for all intents and purposes, runs the Internet. For those content creators that also edit and publish their own websites, a little bit of JavaScript know-how can go a long way.

K

Keyword

Often confused with search term, a keyword is all or any part of a search. For the search term, "how to build your own sistine chapel," Google may remove the following stop words: how, to, your, and own.

That would leave "build," "sistine," "chapel," "build sistine," "build chapel," "build sistine chapel," "sistine chapel," and, "chapel," as keywords.

As search engines index a page, they break it down into keywords to better discover its purpose. When a user performs a search, the search engine helps them find pages that best satisfy their keyword request.

Keyword Stuffing

In the early days of search engines, website owners discovered that they could easily improve their page rankings by repeating target keywords ad nauseam—basically stuffing their content full with unnecessary and often hidden repetitions.

Ranking algorithms easily detect this practice now and offending sites receive penalties.

L

Landing Page

In strict analytics terms, the landing page is the page on our website at which a user begins their session. Whatever page they start on, that page counts as a landing page according to Google Analytics.

However, marketing defines the term more narrowly as a piece of middle-funnel content. From a content creator's perspective, the landing page is one that introduces the reader to something (often the product or service) and ends with a call-to-action. Often times the home page will double as a landing page.

Latency

The time spent loading, buffering, or otherwise waiting for a website's content to appear on screen. Every moment visitors spend waiting for our site negatively impacts their experience and can lead to a bounce.

Latency is highest for visitors appearing on our website for the first time (their browsers have yet to cache our data).

Lead

A lead is any potential customer. Typically, organizations divide leads into categories that convey their likelihood to buy: hot, warm, cold, IQL, MQL, and others.

A great content strategy helps guide our leads along the path from cold to hot to sale to repeat business.

Long-Tail Keywords

Long-tail keywords make up the bulk of searches on the Internet, but their individual search volumes are low compared to short-tailed keywords.

Both marketers and search engines find it easier to determine the Intent of a search when expressed as a long-tail keyword. Long-tail keywords provide more specifics and therefore more insight into what the searcher seeks.

Targeting long-tail keywords results in a higher conversion rate and therefore, ROI.

N

New User Percentage

The percentage of users who began their session as first-time visitors of our site. On established websites, the incoming traffic is usually a strong mix of new and repeat users.

P

Page Value

Google Analytics calculates a page's Page Value by summing its contributions to both revenue and goals, then dividing by the number of unique visitors that page received.

And Google Analytics assigns revenue and goal value contributions to each page when the page took part of a session that led to a goal or a purchase. Page value is a strong indicator of whether a page is valuable to the user and to our success.

Conversely, low value pages with high session counts, bounces, and exit rates may indicate that a page acts as a detractor and requires improvement or pruning.

PageSpeed Insights Tool

A tool provided by Google that analyzes the speed

of any webpage for free. The tool produces a score for both mobile and desktop devices. Mobile devices tend to have limited access to high-speed data and processing power, so the scores for mobile tend to skew lower than those of desktops.

We use this tool to discover potential ways to optimize our site speed and in doing so, improve our user's experience.

Position

The location of a page within a search result for a given keyword. The top-most result sits at position 1, the second at position 2, so on and so forth. Naturally, the lower the page's position, the likelier searchers are to see and click on the page.

Prune

To prune is to remove a piece of content from our website and from search engines. This process requires a bit of legwork and steps must be taken in this order: deindex page URL and content images from all search engines, create a permanent redirect to a new URL, edit or remove links to the content, and finally, delete the page.

R

Redirects (301 and 302)

A redirect is an instruction that diverts both browsers and search engine bots to another page. A 301 redirect indicates that the old URL has permanently moved to a new URL, whereas a 302 indicates that this redirection is only temporary.

We use permanent redirects to guide users and search engine bots to new URLs:

mypage.com/store-page 301 redirected to mypage.com/store.

And we use 302 redirects when a page is down or potentially malfunctioning:

creditchecker.com/check-score 302 redirected

to creditchecker.com/blog/checker-down.

In the former case, the URL was changed to a shorter one, in the latter, the credit score checking page was down and the owner redirected the visitor to a blog post that discussed the outage.

Many, if not all CMS tools permit site owners to create redirects.

Report (Google Analytics)

A report (accessed from the Google Analytics' left-hand menu) typically presents one, but occasionally two data dimensions restricted by segment, date range, and filter.

A report helps us narrow an analytics investigation to a specific variable. For example, if we wanted to learn, "which country contributed most to our revenue in Q1," we would reduce our date range to the 1st of January to the 30th of March, open the Audience Location report, add the Revenue dimension, and lastly, sort the data in descending order by Revenue.

S

Sitemap

Figuratively, a sitemap is a flowchart that defines

every page on our site and the relationship between those pages. Literally, the sitemap is a text file that accomplishes a similar goal that we submit to search engines so they may better navigate our website.

If building a website through a CMS such as WordPress or Squarespace, the CMS dynamically generates the sitemap file for us and we typically find it at the following address:
oursite.com/sitemap.xml

Stop Words

Words so commonly used in a given language that search engines ignore them. In the English language, stop words include how, to, what, when, me, the, in, and many more. As a consequence, excluding stop words from a URL is permissible and often has no impact on a page's ranking.

For example, changing

/what-are-we-having-for-dinner.html to

/having-dinner.html will have little-to-no impact on this page's placement in results for search terms similar to, "what are we having for dinner."

T

Title

The title of a webpage is found within a page's `<title>` tag. Search engines use the title attribute (when found) to identify the result to the user. The title translates to the often blue link that directs users to our page. Titles have no character limits, but search engines will truncate them if necessary.

We use titles to identify our page content and entice users to click our result.

V

Volume
The approximate number of searches a keyword receives every month. When provided by AdWords, the volume is accurate but not entirely precise—values are frequently rounded. However, for those with high ad budgets, AdWords reveals more precise data.

Volume is also based on region as data is collected by country of origin. Sometimes the global volume for a keyword does not reflect its regional popularity.

www.ingramcontent.com/pod-product-compliance
Lightning Source LLC
Chambersburg PA
CBHW070930210326
41520CB00021B/6877